Twayne's English Authors Series

EDITOR OF THIS VOLUME

Sylvia E. Bowman

INDIANA UNIVERSITY

Giles and Phineas Fletcher

TEAS 225

GILES AND PHINEAS FLETCHER

By FRANK S. KASTOR

Wichita State University

TWAYNE PUBLISHERS

A DIVISION OF G. K. HALL & CO., BOSTON

Library of Congress Cataloging in Publication Data

Kastor, Frank S   1933 -
  Giles and Phineas Fletcher.

  (Twayne's English authors series ; TEAS 225)
  Bibliography: p. 157 - 58
  Includes index.
    1. Fletcher, Giles, 1588? - 1623—Criticism and interpre-
tation.   2.   Fletcher, Phineas, 1582 - 1650—Criticism and inter-
pretation.   I.   Title.
PR2272.K3   1978   821'.3'09   77-21035
ISBN 0-8057-6696-0

This book is dedicated with love
to my mother, Rebecca Sullivan Kastor,
and to my sons, JaCaeber, Mark, and Harlan Kastor.

Contents

About the Author

Frank Kastor is the author also of *Milton and the Literary Satan* (1974) and articles, reviews, and critical studies about different aspects of English and American literature, which have appeared in *Huntington Library Quarterly, Anglia, Journal of English and Germanic Philology, English Language Notes, The Personalist,* and *Kansas Quarterly.* He has concentrated his research and study mostly on Renaissance and modern literature; and he has taught at the University of Illinois (M.A.), the University of California, Berkeley (Ph.D.), the University of Southern California, La Laguna Universidad, Spain (as a Fulbright Lecturer), and Northern Illinois University. He is now Professor of English at Wichita State University, Wichita, Kansas.

Preface

Frederick S. Boas concluded his Preface to *The Poetical Works of Giles and Phineas Fletcher* (1908), the standard works in two volumes, with the following remark: "I hope that [my scholarly editorial labors] may lay the foundation for a more critical and considered estimate of [the Fletchers'] poetic merits than has hitherto been possible." My own hope is that this critical study of the literature of the two poet-priest brothers may in some way fulfill Boas' hope. For until now there has never, in fact, been a thorough, book-length critical investigation of the two poet-brothers.

The only book about either man—A. B. Langdale, *Phineas Fletcher: Man of Letters, Science and Divinity* (1937)—is a valuable biography, but it is in no way a critical analysis of the works, which serve mainly as source material for the author's splendid biography. Aside from Grosart's nineteenth-century biographical defense of them in his edition, H. E. Cory's sixty-page study, "Spenser, The School of the Fletchers, and Milton," (1912), Grundy's discussion in *The Spenserian Poets* (1969), several doctoral dissertations, and half a dozen brief articles and notes on each, one finds only passing remarks and brief comments about them in literary histories and in special studies of the seventeenth-century and Renaissance writers.

My aims are 1) to provide the first systematic and thorough critical study of the total writings of each; 2) to trace the development of each writer; 3) to characterize and separate Giles from Phineas; 4) to review their critical reception through the centuries; and, finally, 5) to synthesize and build upon the scholarship and criticism that have been devoted to them in the past.

In short, in this study I seek finally to increase our understanding of the work of these poet-brothers and, hopefully, to fulfill Boas' old request "for a more critical and considered estimate of their poetic merits"—a request that has remained unfulfilled for much too long.

I wish to thank Cambridge University Press for their kind permission to quote fully and amply from the Boas edition, the National Endowment for the Humanities for a research grant supporting part of this study, and my colleagues, Professors Seymour Gross, Gerald Hoag, Dorothy Walters, for reading parts of the manuscript with helpful eyes.

Frank S. Kastor

Wichita State University

Chronology

CHAPTER 1

The Literary Fletchers

THE Fletchers hold a singular place in the history of
English literature. Giles Fletcher, Sr., his sons Phineas and
Giles, Jr., and their first cousin John Fletcher, the poet-dramatist,
comprise England's largest, most significant family of writers. As a
prominent nineteenth-century scholar wrote, "the family of
Fletcher was rendered illustrious . . . by a constellation of poetic
power."[1] Furthermore, their lives span a most important hundred
years in English cultural history, 1550 - 1650, which includes the
Renaissance, the Reformation, the revolutionary Civil Wars, and
two great periods of English literature—Elizabethan and Jacobean
(Queen Elizabeth, 1558 - 1603; King James, 1603 - 1625). The
careers and writings of the literary Fletchers, which involve two
generations, perfectly illustrate some of the most fundamental
literary patterns and characteristics of the two periods.

I *The Older Generation: Elizabethans*

The careers of Giles Fletcher, Sr. (1548 - 1611) and his older
brother Richard (1545 - 96) were connected with the court of
Elizabeth.[2] The court was not only the seat of power and culture,
but also the center of the English literary world. Richard, the father
of John the dramatist, like his own father, went from Cambridge
University into the ministry. He established his family at Cranbrook, Kent, the family seat, and his ministry nearby at Rye and
in the area. In 1586, when Mary Queen of Scots was imprisoned
at Fotheringay Castle in Richard's diocese and was awaiting her execution, Richard's performance of church duties and offices for the
Catholic monarch won him the esteem of Queen Elizabeth herself.
Thereafter he became in rapid order her own chaplain, then Bishop
of Bristol, and finally Bishop of London in 1594. During this time,
Richard lived in London; he regularly attended the Queen at court;

and he was apparently a loyal party man, a middle-of-the-road curate, and useful to the Queen in the difficult administration of church governance and politics.

Richard Fletcher's rapid rise. to lofty position and influence illustrates the essential attraction of a court-oriented career. However, his even more rapid fall from favor—due apparently to the Calvinistic slant of his Lambeth Articles and a second marriage which angered the Queen—illustrates also the dangers of that type of career. It is probably symbolic that, despite the many properties and rewards of his office, the settlement of his estate in 1596 left his heirs actually in debt to the Crown. If Richard exemplifies one type of career that was open to bright, middle-class, Elizabethan Englishmen, his younger brother Giles, Sr., graphically illustrates another: one that involved the Elizabethan literary scene.

Giles Fletcher, Sr., father of Phineas and Giles, Jr., could be described as almost the quintessence of what the English, Renaissance society and culture of the sixteenth century were destined to produce in terms of a literary career. Giles, Sr. received the best of Renaissance humanistic education at Eton and Cambridge. At King's College, Cambridge, from 1565 - 79, he became in rapid succession Scholar, Fellow, Bachelor of Arts, Master of Arts, and Deputy Orator of the University. In 1576, in the reformation spirit, Giles, Sr. led a group which formally accused the provost of King's College of maladministration and of misapplication of college statutes. The charges were acted upon unfavorably by the Chancellor of the University, the great Lord Burghley, which apparently led to Giles' forfeiture of fellowship, his living, and eventually his whole career at Cambridge. Giles, who quickly switched to the study of law, attained a Doctorate of Civil Law in 1581. In that year, he also married Joan Sheafe, the daughter of a rich and influential merchant from Cranbrook, and commenced his new career in public affairs. Apparently as a result of the connections of his brother Richard at Elizabeth's court and his family's influence, Giles obtained a series of public offices: Commissary to the Chancellor of Ely, visiting Commissioner to the church of Chichester, then Chancellor (1582), member of Parliament for Winchelsea (1585), Remembrancer or Secretary of London in 1586. He was sent to Scotland, Germany, and Russia for several years in various ambassadorial capacities for Elizabeth's court. In the 1590s, he returned to promising civil positions in England. However, after the death of his brother Richard in 1596, Giles' career and fortunes floundered. He was saved from arrest over his brother's indebted estate by the Earl of Essex, that bold, dashing favorite of Queen Elizabeth. But Giles' career, along with many others, sank in the debacle of the Essex rebellion in 1599. Fletcher was implicated, jailed, and disenfranchised politically. Although his family finally worked his release and although he lived eleven more years, his public career and aspirations (like Edmund Spenser's) ended with the century in 1599.

Giles Fletcher's writing career also ended with the close of the sixteenth century, and his works are related closely to the tastes and fashions of the court world of Elizabeth. As early as 1563 he began making public his Latin verses: in a collection from students of Eton to the Queen; a poem prefixed to John Foxe's *Acts and Monuments* (1570 ed.); another with Walter Haddon's *Poems* (1576); others with Robert Carr's *Demosthenes* (1571), in Raphael Holinshed's *Chronicles*, and in a Cambridge volume of 1587 memorializing Sir Philip Sidney's death. The writing of Latin verse meant more than schoolboy exercises in language and composition to the Elizabethan: it was an act of participation in the great classical world of letters as well as the work of Humanists, of educated men, and of the courtiers around Elizabeth to whom such preoccupations were the necessary adjuncts of the well-rounded gentleman.

Today, Giles Fletcher, Sr., is probably best known for his sonnet cycle *Licia* (1593). The sonnet was easily the single most popular short lyric poem during the reigns of Queen Elizabeth and her successor James. The cycle of sonnets (a diary in verse of some amorous relationship) became fashionable in the 1590s. The perfect pattern of an Elizabethan courtier, Sir Philip Sidney himself started the fad with his *Astrophel and Stella* (1591); and Samuel Daniel, Giles Fletcher, Sr., Thomas Lodge, Edmund Spenser, and William Shakespeare quickly followed suit. Although much has been written about the Courtly Love sentiments and themes expressed in Elizabethan sonnets and cycles like *Licia,* they also reflect the perilous and capricious existence of those who, like their authors, aspired to court careers. The suffering of unrequited love; the faithfulness of the servant-lover through every kind of trial and tribulation; the cruelty, capriciousness, and lack of either pity or reward for constancy; the moments of exaltation, hope, and idealism punctured by despair—such are the themes of the sonneteers. As the great patrons like Lord Burghley, the Earl of Leicester, and the Earl of Essex rose and fell in favor like courtly lovers, so too did their retainers like Giles Fletcher, Sr., and his brother Richard.

The adventure of travel—the fascination of new or exotic lands—was strong also in the age and especially at the court which was financing much of that travel. Giles' prose account of his experiences in Russia is, therefore, as court-oriented as his sonnet cycle. *Of the Russe Common Wealth; or, Manner of Government by the Russe Emperour (commonly called the Emperour of Moskovia), with the Manners and Fashions of the People of the Country* (1591) was, in fact, dedicated by Giles to Queen Elizabeth. It appeared in the same year as Sir Walter Raleigh's *A Report . . . of the Flight about the Isle of Azores* and a few years before Raleigh's *The Discovery of the large, rich and beautiful Empire of Guiana*. An abridged version appeared also in the most famous collection of such materials, Richard Hakluyt's *Principal Navigations, Voyages, and Discoveries of the English Nation* (1589 - 1600).

Another characteristic of the 1580s and 1590s which finds voice in Giles' account of Russia is the court's interest in history, particularly in English history. However, this interest is more obviously manifest in Giles' narrative poem, "Rising the Crown of Richard the Third" (1593). It and Daniel's *History of the Civil Wars;* Michael Drayton's poem *The Baron's Wars;* the numerous English chronicle plays of William Shakespeare, Christopher Marlowe, George Peele, Robert Greene; and the actual histories and chronicles by Raphael Holinshed, John Stowe, and William Camden are but a few additional examples of the age's widespread fascination with history. In the 1590s, Giles also submitted to Elizabeth a design for an extensive history of her reign in Latin. He fell from favor, however, before it was approved.

The career of Giles Fletcher, Sr.—lawyer, civil servant, member of parliament, ambassador, historian, courtier, poet, free-lance writer—illustrates the basic pattern of the leading literary figures of the Elizabethan age. Sir Philip Sidney (b. 1554) has been considered the perfect Elizabethan courtier—the perfect embodiment of Castiglione's ideal courtier. However, Edmund Spenser (b. 1552), Giles Fletcher, Sr. (b. 1548), Walter Raleigh (b. 1552), John Lyly (b. 1554), Thomas Lodge (b. 1557), Samuel Daniel (b. 1562), or Michael Drayton (b. 1563) are more typical because they represent the emerging middle class; Sidney, the declining aristocracy.

This generation of writers shared many features. They were all educated at Oxford or Cambridge at about the same time. They were all trained for public, court-oriented careers, which they undertook. Their literature emanated from and reflects the world, atmosphere, fashions, and fads of Elizabeth's court. They all were professional writers, patronized by court or courtiers; none made a living directly from writing. The prototype of the pattern was Sidney; the best poet was Spenser; the most typical was probably Giles Fletcher, Sr. They produced a remarkable body of literature in a very few years. In fact, aside from a notable body of public drama (also produced largely by middle-class, university men), the body of literature they wrote is what one studies today as Elizabethan literature.

II *The Younger Generation: Jacobeans*

The second generation of literary Fletchers (John, Phineas, and Giles, Jr.,) are as related in career and letters to Jacobean England as their fathers were to Elizabethan. John Fletcher (1579 - 1625), son of Bishop Richard Fletcher, became a dramatist—a new kind of literary career which had opened in England in his lifetime as a result of the opening of public theaters. His career also illustrates the consequences of being a younger son of a dignitary whose sudden worldly fall left an indebted estate, for he was the "John Fletcher of London" who became "a pensioner at Bene't College, Cambridge" (his father had been president of it) and a Bible clerk there in the 1590s. However, after his father's fall, nothing more is heard of him until he appears as a dramatist in London who was working and living with Francis Beaumont (1584 - 1616).

As a team, Beaumont and Fletcher proved the most popular and successful collaborators on the Jacobean stage from about 1608 to 1616. John Aubrey wrote that they shared a "wonderful consimility of phansy"; that "they lived together on the Bank side, not far from the Play-House [Southwark, near the Globe], both batchelors"; and that they shared everything. Together, they wrote about seven plays. Fletcher, who wrote about fifteen others by himself, also collaborated with the other leading dramatists of the day: Philip Massinger (chiefly), Ben Jonson, Cyril Tourneur, Nathan Field, Thomas Middleton, Samuel Rowley, James Shirley, and William Shakespeare. In short, John Fletcher was a full-time professional dramatist who, by all accounts, was notably successful.

Yet such a career, despite its newness, glamour, and the fact that men with backgrounds much like John's had created the new public theater, was not socially acceptable to the middle class. John's family seem to have disowned him; and his uncle, Giles Fletcher and his cousins Phineas and Giles apparently had nothing more to do with him.

John Fletcher was born just after the first public theaters were built in London, The Theatre and The Curtain (1576 - 77). During the 1590s, his teen-age, Fletcher would have had half a dozen London theaters to choose from and considerable motivation to attend them regularly, for the public stage was not only one of the newest and most exciting aspects of London life, it was also the cheapest and most flourishing form of popular entertainment.

The tremendous variety, vitality, and theatricality of the public stage was in large part the product of young men with backgrounds much like that of John Fletcher; and they are usually called the University Wits. These young men—Marlowe, Greene, Peele, Nash, Kyd—had arrived in London from the universities and created a new career. Professional dramatists and free-lance writers, they combined their formal education in classical literature and their experience in university drama with the demands of public entertainment and with the experience of the professional actors whom they joined. Within twenty years, they produced one of the great periods in theatrical history; their labors prepared the way for Shakespeare's plays.

John Fletcher began his playwright's career during the reign of James I (1603 - 25) when the Jacobean theater world that he entered was rapidly transforming its Elizabethan foundation. For one thing, although Shakespeare was still in his prime, a whole new generation of dramatists had replaced the University Wits. These were the schoolmates or close contemporaries of not only John Fletcher but also his cousins Giles and Phineas. Ben Jonson (1573 - 1637) was the dominating and central figure in most ways; but Thomas Heywood (1573 - 1641), Thomas Dekker (1572 - 1632), John Marston (1575 - 1634), George Chapman (1559 - 1634), Thomas Middleton (1580 - 1627), John Webster (1580 - 1625), Cyril Tourneur (1580 - 1626), Philip Massinger (1583 - 1640), and John Ford (1586 - 1655), as well as Francis Beaumont and John Fletcher, formed now the undisputed staple of the stage. Furthermore, by 1605, London, with one hundred sixty thousand inhabitants, had a dozen theaters—a far better ratio than most English or American cities can claim today even with cinemas.

With the heightened dramatic activity, however, came new directions—new mood, new temper, and new atmosphere. At the turn of the century a so-called 'War of the Theatres" occurred between the old and new playwrights, as if to symbolize the new directions and foreshadow the social history of the seventeenth century.

As with most cultural phenomena, the changes apparent in Jacobean drama reflect and involve larger social forces at work. In fact, important changes, already seen on the Continent, were sweeping England. During the seventeenth century, England underwent the most violent, revolutionary changes in its history; these affected all spheres of political, economic, religious, cultural, social, intellectual, and artistic activity; and these formed the milieu out of which Phineas, Giles, Jr., and John Fletcher wrote.

CHAPTER 2

Giles Fletcher, Jr.

I Life[1]

THE known facts about the life and career of Giles Fletcher, Jr. form an unfortunately sketchy portrait. Thomas Fuller, his seventeenth-century biographer, provides a starting point: "Giles Fletcher was born in this city [London] son to Giles Fletcher, doctor in law, and ambassador into Russia." Giles, Jr., the third child and the second son, was born some time between the Novembers of 1585 and 1586 while his father was in London as a member of Parliament. His mother, Joan Sheafe, was a daughter of the Sheafe family from Cranbrook, Kent, the Fletcher family seat. Young Giles, Jr. appears to have divided his early years between London and Cranbrook as his father's duties abroad and at home dictated.

He was educated at Westminster School, London, and Trinity College, Cambridge. In late 1602 or early 1603, he joined his elder brother Phineas at Cambridge and commenced a university career which lasted fifteen years. His literary activity, poetry mainly, began at once and formed a substantial part of those years and that career. In 1603, both he and his brother Phineas achieved distinction by having their poems about the death of Queen Elizabeth selected for inclusion in the University commemorative anthology, *Sorrowes Joy* (Cambridge, 1603). From 1603 to 1610, the two brothers were deeply and mutually involved in writing poetry, and they also became the nucleus of a literary coterie which slowly grew in size and influence at Cambridge.[2]

In 1610, Cambridge University Press published what was to become Giles' major work, *Christ's Victorie and Triumph*, a sacred heroic poem or epyllion in four books. This poem was to prove significant in the literary history of the century and the basis of his subsequent reputation as a poet; for, among other things, it clearly and heavily influenced works of John Milton.[3] In 1612, several of Giles' English and Latin elegiac poems on the death of Prince Henry appeared in another commemorative anthology from Cambridge, *Epicedium Cantabrigiense*. He also edited and published a manuscript by Nathaniel Pownall, his first cousin and a fellow student who had just died, *The Young divines Apologie for his continuance in the University with certain Meditations*.

At Cambridge, Giles, Jr. received a Scholarship (1605), completed a Bachelor of Arts degree (1606), became a minor Fellow at Trinity (1608), and then a Reader in Greek Grammar (1615). In 1615, his patron Thomas Nevile died, and soon afterward Giles left Cambridge. In 1617, he became the rector of a small parrish in Suffolk. He returned to Cambridge long enough to complete a Bachelor of Divinity degree in 1618. The next year he became the rector of the country church at Alderton, Suffolk. He died in 1623 the year of publication of his final work, a book of devotional prose, *The Reward of the Faithful*, the title of which forms a not unfitting epitaph.

II   *Patterns*

Giles' life, despite its brevity (thirty-seven years) and the general paucity of known external details, exemplifies some rather significant career patterns for seventeenth-century poets and writers. It demonstrates again how directly systems of patronage in Tudor-Stuart politics could and did affect all levels of a man's career. As a graduate of Westminster School, Giles had been eligible for one of three scholarships to Trinity College, Cambridge, which had been established by Queen Elizabeth in 1560. Doctor Thomas Nevile, Master of Trinity College, as well as Dean of Canterbury, apparently awarded these scholarships when it pleased him. In 1607, when King James himself directed that scholars from Westminster completing Bachelor of Arts degrees at Trinity should receive first priority on these fellowships. Nevile objected, petitioned the Chancellor for review, and finally in 1608 refused to make the Westminster appointments.

However, in 1608 Giles did receive a minor appointment as a fellow; and his gratitude to Nevile, who might have been a distant relative by marriage, for this personal patronage is unequivocal. In 1612, Giles dedicated *Christ's Victory and Triumph* to Nevile and in the "Epistle Dedicatory" wrote: "in cambridge: in which beeing placed by your onely favour, most freely, without either any meanes from other, or any desert in my selfe, beeing not able to doe more, I could doe no lesse, then acknowledge that debt, which I shall never be able to pay." This statement he enlarged upon as follows: "I cannot but next unto God, for ever acknowledge myselfe most bound unto the hand of God, (I meane yourselfe) that reacht downe, as it were out of heave, unto me, a benefit of that nature, and price, then which, I could wish none, (onely heaven itselfe excepted) either more fruitful, and contenting for the time that is now present, or more comfortable, and encouraging for the time that is yet to come."[4]

The dedication clearly indicates that direct, personal patronage rather than university statutes or innate abilities produced Giles' fellowship and maintained his living at Trinity. Surely the preferment accounts not only for Scholarship, Fellowship, and Readership but for other honors, such as the one he shared with Senior Bursar, Thomas Fortho, of carrying college and university letters in person to King James and to Prince Charles in 1615. Patronage clearly provided the basis of his college career, which in turn formed the foundation of his literary career; for after the death of Thomas Nevile in May, 1615, as has been noted, Giles Fletcher's Cambridge career soon faltered, then ended.

The uncertainties of dependence upon one patron must have been clear to Giles for his own father and uncle had provided more than sufficient examples. However, within a year of Nevile's death, Giles secured new patronage and a new position, and embarked upon a new career. From the Fletcher family records, we learn that Sir Roger Townshend and his uncle, Sir Francis Bacon, Lord Viscount and Lord Chancellor of England, "presented Mr. Gyles Fletcher of Trin: Coll: Camb. to the rectory of Helmingsham in Suffolk," the living from which they owned.[5] Giles left Cambridge early in 1617 to assume his new position and duties in that remote hamlet. Of his general qualification for such a position, Thomas Fuller says: "one equally beloved of the Muses and the Graces, having a sanctified wit; witness his worthy poem, intituled 'Christ's Victory,' made by him being but bachelor of arts, discovering the piety of a saint, and the divinity of a doctor. He afterward applied himself to school divinity (cross to the grain of his genius as some conceive), and attained to good skill therein. When he preached at Saint Mary's his prayer before his sermon usually consisted of one entire allegory, not driven, but led on, most proper in all particulars."

However, Giles remained in that post less than one year; why he left so quickly remains unclear. It has been speculated that coolness between himself and Sir Lionel Tollemachie and his family, who dominated Helmingsham society, might have caused his departure. Perhaps new opportunity arose at Trinity College, for he returned there in early 1618 as Lector Graecae Linguae. More likely, both this appointment and the Bachelor of Divinity degree which he completed within a year (1619) were prerequisites for a new position. At any event, his new patrons, Sir Roger Townshend and Sir Francis Bacon, presented him in 1619 with another benefice or living, at the somewhat larger town of Alderton, Suffolk. In the "Epistle Dedicatory" to Giles' prose work, *The Reward of the Faithful* (1623), which he dedicated to Townshend, he comments upon the matter: "Your most noble and learned Uncle, the Right Honorable Francis Lord Verulam, Viscount Saint Albones, my free and very Honourable Benefactor, whose Gift, as it was worthy of bestowing, so was it speedily sent, and not tediously sued for; Honourably given not bought with shame, to one whom he never knew or saw, but only heard kindly slaundered with a good report of others, and opinion conceived by himselfe of sufficiencie and worth. For by your Favours I confesse, my estate is something, but the sence of my povertie much more increased."[6]

Although Giles was clearly grateful for the patronage, it appears from the scanty evidence that he did not flourish in the living. In fact, he died within four years. The nagging undertone, for example, in the line, "but the sence of my povertie much more increased," catches a recurrent note in the writings of the last years. During these years, he also married, but only Anne's given name is known. She outlived him and married the Reverend John Ramsey, minister of East Rudham, Norfolk, who supplied Fuller with much of his information about Giles' life; and Fuller writes about the years and conditions at Alderton that: "He was at last (by exchange of his living) settled in Suffolk, which hath the best and worst air in England; best about Bury, and worst on the sea-side, where Master Fletcher was beneficed. His clownish and low-parted parishioners (having nothing but their shoes high about them) valued not their pastor according to his worth; which disposed him to melancholy, and hastened his disolution. I behold the life of this learned poet, like those half verses in Virgil's *Aeneid,* broken off in the middle, seeing he might have doubled his days according to the ordinary course of nature; whose death happened about the year 162[3]," at age thirty-seven.

The tone of Giles' final piece of writing, the "Epistle Dedicatory"
to *The Reward of the Faithful,* seems to support Fuller's contention
about melancholy and even about actual dissolution. An unusual
heaviness of tone, a recurrent sense of world weariness, and a distinct emphasis upon illness and physical decay pervades the following typical passage:

So fast grow the ill weedes of Nature when Nature it Selfe decayes in us.
Now wee cannot bee ignorant that in the very Spring of nature, these three
strong infirmities were seeded in us. The first upon the effacing of God's
Image, a dimme eye-sight or darknesse in our soule: the second a lame
hand or idlenesse in the body, which grew when Mortalitie first broke in
upon us, and left our nature consumed of that first-borne strength it then
flowrished with: bringing in upon our labour an accursed sweat, upon our
sweat, weariness, and consequently faynting, and languishing the whole
body with unrest, and disease.

However, the fact that Giles was one of the Faithful to the end can
be little doubted.

III   *A New Career Pattern*

Even Giles' earliest writings present ample evidence of his very
clear and self-conscious dedication of himself to religion—both as
man and poet. In the dedicatory verse to *Christ's Victorie* in 1609 -
10, Phineas makes special note of it; and Fuller descibes the young
poet as having "the piety of a saint, and the divinity of a doctor."
Giles' "Epistle dedicatory" to the 1612 edition of Nathaniel Pownall's *The Young Divines Apologie* contains a number of statements
that indicate the kind of career Giles was anticipating. In the
dedication to John King, Pownall's patron and the Bishop of London, Giles states that he wishes to carry on Pownall's work of "doing
the church of God some service." The relationship of this service to
literature and learning is made equally clear when Giles speaks, for
example, of his dead cousin, "The author," as "The swan that,
before his death, sung this divine song." He notes how the young
divine's learning, modesty, piety, knowledge, and industry are now
"not with him in his grave, but in these immortal monuments of the
presse, the living Tombes proper to dead learning, wherein these
flowers may live, though their roots be withered, and though the
trunk be dead, the branches flowrish."[7]
All the evidence suggests that Giles was self-consciously develop-

ing his career as both poet and priest—probably as poet-priest. The "Epistle," which deals intra-relatedly with clergy, authors, learning, and books, is written in the most distinctly literary manner of the day, the "grand" or "ciceronian" style:

Ten yeares had hee lived in the Universitie, eight languages had hee learnt, and taught his tongue so many several waies by which to expresse a good heart; watching often, daily exercising, always studying, in a word, making an end of himselfe in an over-fervant desire to benefit others; and yet, after hee had, as it wear out of himself, sweat out all this oyle for his lampe, after hee had with the sunne ran so many heavenly races, and when the sunne was laided abed by his labours, after hee had burnt out so many candles to give his mind light . . . so as to be of the Angells of God.

He could have also been writing about himself, about his life at Cambridge, which was centered in university and church.

Ten years later, Giles speaks in *The Reward of the Faithful*, against the kinds of literary career that had been undertaken by his own father and his cousin, John: "Among the crowde of this ranke (idlers) wee may thrust in our idle pamphleteers and loose poets, no better than the priests of Venus, with the rabble of stage-players, battelers and circumferaneous fiddlers and brokers: all which if they were cleane taken out of the world there would bee little misse of them." This judgment seems less the voice of a reactionary country priest, jealous and frustrated by his life, than that of one who "Proov'd the Muses not to Venus Bound," as Phineas said of him.[8]

In fact, Giles' career can be viewed as a prototype of a new pattern in England. Ranged behind him as poet-priests are some of the leading literary figures of the seventeenth century: John Donne, George Herbert, Phineas Fletcher, Richard Crashaw, Robert Herrick, Thomas Fuller, Jeremy Taylor, John Bunyan, and Robert Burton, to mention a few. The new pattern reflects a shift from careers centered at court like his own father's to those centered in the university and in the church. The full effects upon literature of such a shift are obviously complex and difficult to isolate, especially since these writers lived through one of the most turbulent periods of English history, a period in which all institutions, including university and church, were torn with controversy, strife, and antagonism. However, it is clear that such poet-priests helped produce yet another great age of literature—an age different from that of their fathers and one noted for some of the world's finest religious poetry. The career and works of John Milton, the greatest and most

representative writer of the century who had been destined for a
church career, clearly exemplifies this pattern.

IV   *Early Poetry: "A Canto Upon the Death of Eliza"*

That Giles Fletcher's poem "A Canto Upon the Death of Eliza"
should have been included in a volume like *Sorrowes Joy,* the university's official gift in 1603 to the new monarch, King James,
suggests that the seventeen-year-old sophomore had already gained
some standing as a poet at college and university. Although Giles'
poem may be the work of an apprentice poet, it is far from that of a
beginner and warrants a complete reading:

A Canto Upon the Death of Eliza[9]

(1)

The Earely Houres were readie to unlocke
   The doore of Morne, to let abroad the Day,
When sad *Ocyroe* sitting on a rocke,
Hemmd in with teares, not glassing as they say
Shee woont, her damaske beuties (when to play
   She bent her looser fancie) in the streame,
   That sudding on the rocke, would closely seeme
To imitate her whitenesse with his frothy creame.

(2)

But hanging from the stone her carefull head,
That shewed (for griefe had made it so to shew)
A stone it selfe, thus onely differed,
That those without, these streames within did flow,
Both ever ranne, yet never lesse did grow,
   And tearing from her head her amber haires,
   Whose like or none, or onely Phaebus weares,
Shee strowd thē on the flood to waite upō her teares.

(3)

About her many Nymphes sate weeping by,
That when shee sang were woont to daunce & leape.
And all the grasse that round about did lie,
Hung full of teares, as if that meant to weepe,
Whilest, th' undersliding streames did softly creepe,
   And clung about the rocke with winding wreath,
   To heare a *Canto* of Elizaes death:
Which thus poore nymph shee sung, whilest sorrowe lent her breath.

(4)

Tell me ye blushing currols that bunch out,
To cloathe with beuteous red your ragged sire,
So let the sea-greene mosse curle round about
With soft embrace (as creeping vines doe wyre
Their loved Elmes) your sides in rosie tyre,
    So let the ruddie vermeyle of your cheeke
    Make staind carnations fresher liveries seeke,
So let your braunched armes grow crooked, smooth, & sleeke.

(5)

So from your growth late be you rent away,
And hung with silver bels and whistles shrill,
Unto those children be you given to play
where blest Eliza raignd: so never ill
Betide your canes nor them with breaking spill,
    Tell me if some uncivill hand should teare
    Your branches hence, and place them otherwhere;
Could you still grow, & such fresh crimson ensignes beare?

(6)

Tell me sad Philomele that yonder sit'st
Piping thy songs unto the dauncing twig,
And to the waters fall thy musicke fit'st,
So let the friendly prickle never digge
Thy watchfull breast with wound or small or bigge,
    Whereon thou lean'st, so let the hissing snake
    Sliding with shrinking silence never take
Th'unwarie foote, whilst thou perhaps hangst halfe awake.

(7)

So let the loathed lapwing when her nest
Is stolne away, not as shee uses, flie,
Cousening the searcher of his promisd feast,
But widdowd of all hope still *Itis* crie,
And nought but *Itis, Itis*, till shee die.
    Say sweetest querister of the airie quire
    Doth not thy *Tereu, Tereu* then expire,
When winter robs thy house of all her greene attire?

(8)

Tell me ye velvet headed violets
That fringe the crooked banke with gawdie blewe,
So let with comely grace your prettie frets
Be spread, so let a thousand *Zephyrs* sue

To kisse your willing heads, that seeme t'eschew
   Their wanton touch with maiden modestie,
   So let the silver dewe but lightly lie
Like little watrie worlds within your azure skie,

(9)

So when your blazing leaves are broadly spread
Let wandring nymphes gather you in their lapps,
And send you where Eliza lieth dead,
To strow the sheete that her pale bodie wraps,
Aie me in this I envie your good haps:
   Who would not die, there to be buried?
   Say if the sunne denie his beames to shedde
Upon your living stalkes, grow you not withered?

(10)

Tell me thou wanton brooke, that slip'st away
T'avoid the straggling bankes still flowing cling,
So let thy waters cleanely tribute pay
Unmixt with mudde unto the sea your king,
So never let your streames leave murmuring
   Until they steale by many a secret furt
   To kisse those walls that built Elizaes court,
Drie you not when your mother springs are choakt with durt?

(11)

Yes you all say, and I say with you all,
Naught without cause of joy can joyous bide,
Then me unhappie nymph whome the dire fall
Of my joyes spring, But there aye me shee cried,
And spake no more, for sorrow speech denied.
   And downe into her watrie lodge did goe;
   The very waters when shee sunke did showe
With many wrinckled ohs they sympathiz'd her woe.

(12)

The sunne in mourning cloudes inveloped
Flew fast into the westearne world to tell
Newes of her death. Heaven it selfe sorrowed
With teares that to the earthes danke bosome fell;
But when the next Aurora gan to deale
   Handfuls of roses fore the teame of day
   A sheapheard drove his flocke by chance that way
& made the nymph to dance that mourned yesterday.

                         G. Fletcher. Trinit.

That Giles should have written a very Elizabethan poem on the occasion of Elizabeth's death probably strikes the modern reader as appropriate. However, that the poem is without deep feeling, is in fact almost totally impersonal, undoubtedly troubles this reader far more than it would have his Elizabethan counterpart. Both the death and coronation of a monarch were public events, and "The Queen is dead! Long live the King!" rang out all over England in 1603. The twofold paradoxical direction stated in the volume's full title clearly suggests the avoidance of public grief: *Sorrowes Joy, Or A Lamentation for our late deceased Soveraigne Elizabeth, with a triumph for the prosperous succession of our gratious King, James.* In the poem, this paradox becomes transformed into the Nymphes "woont to daunce & leape" who were weeping over "Eliza's death" (st. 3, 1 - 2) until "A sheapheard [James] drove his flocke by chance that way / & made the nymph to dance that mourned yesterday" (st. 12).

The form that Giles uses to memorialize the death is that of a formal song (Canto) of lament by a mythological figure, and the setting is some nonspecified rock by the side of some nondesignated pastoral stream. Ocyroe, the water nymph with prophetic powers described in Ovid's *Metamorphosis* (2:633ff), sits surrounded by Nymphes (sts. 1 - 3); and the body of the poem (sts. 4 - 11) is her lament. The same ideal pastoral world and mode of writing appears often in Elizabethan literature of which Spenser's *Shepherd's Calendar* and Sidney's *Arcadia* are especially relevant examples; they both appear to have influenced Giles, Jr. generally and this poem especially. The pastoral world formed a too substantial voice in classical writings—the educational foundation of all Renaissance students—not to be echoed in Renaissance literature. For the generations of schoolboys like Giles who were long on classical reading but short on extracurricular experiences, the extensive borrowing from classical mythology and modes, is easily understandable. More importantly, to present their feelings and ideas in such terms was to join the classical tradition, *the* literary tradition—to become fraternal with Vergil, Theocritus, Bion, Ovid, and with their contemporary followers like Sidney and Spenser.

"Eliza" also reflects a kind of formula for the fashionable, "well-made" poem of the day. The relationship of music and poetry is fundamental to that formula: what Milton described a few years later as those "Sphere-born harmonious Sisters, Voice and Verse" ("At A Solemn Music"). Parts of nature—flowers, stream, trees, birds—are solicited ("Tell me. . .") for their feelings and called to action ("So let . . . "). Mythological figures, references, and allusions, as well as personification and pathetic fallacy, appear prominently. However, description, highly rhetorical description, forms the center of the poem. Rhetoric was, of course, one of the three main subjects studied throughout a schoolboy's career during the Renaissance. Grammar and Logic were the others. The student's textbooks were as filled with the "gems and rubies" of rhetoric as were the subsequent poems, plays, and prose works that he wrote. Shakespeare and the other Elizabethan "worthies" were notably extravagant in this respect.

Most stanzas in the poem turn upon the rhetorical construction of direct address: question ("tell me") followed by command ("So let"). The other most common rhetorical devices used in the poem are the following: paradox, "That those without, these streames within did flow" (2:4); antithesis, "Both ever ranne, yet never lesse did grow" (2:5); personification (sts. 1, 6, 8, for example); pathetic fallacy (throughout); inversion, "Yes you all say, and I say with you all (11:1); alliteration, assonance, consonance, and other patterns of sound repetition ("with winding wreath," "So let the loathéd lapwing when," "Say sweetest querister of the airie quire," and so forth).

The style is not only rhetorical, it is consciously enriched and fashioned into a distinct poetic diction. For instance, there is heavy reliance on adjectives; every noun seems to have at least one or two. This device adds color and sensuousness; it also underscores how important the rhetorical device of description is to this poem: "So let the ruddie vermeyle of your cheeke / Make stained carnations fresher liveries seeke" (4:6 - 7). In this poetry, which labors to be rich, sensuous, even luxuriant in language, emotion and thought are consistently sacrificed to "poetic effect," to memorable lines or stanzas. Behind the poem is that recurrent Renaissance notion that poetry is prose dressed up in verse form. Two decades later, another young Cambridge sophomore, John Milton, expressed the idea as follows:

> And from thy wardrobe bring thy chiefest treasure;
> Not those new fangled toys, and trimming slight
> Which takes our late fantastics with delight,
> But cull those richest Robes, and gay'st attire
> Which deepest Spirits, and choicest Wits desire:
> I have some naked thoughts that rove about

And loudly knock to have their passage out;
And weary of their place do only stay
Till thou hast deck't them in thy best array.

("At A Vacation Exercise")

Ben Jonson, writing about Shakespeare, said "though the Poet's matter, Nature be / His Art doth give the fashion"; and he added, "a good Poet's made, as well as born." Behind these two statements is the view of the poet as craftsman, maker, and artisan.

The other major Renaissance notion of the poet, taken also from the classical tradition, sees the poet as seer, prophet, or bard. Sidney's *Defense of Poesy*, the *locus classicus* of English Renaissance critical theory, discusses at length the "poietes" (Greek from *poiein*, to make) and the *vates* (Latin for prophet or poet). The two notions of the poet as "vates" and "poietes" were not contradictory. However, Giles' "Eliza" bears all the signs of the "poietes" and none of the signs of the *vates* at work. Giles appears more concerned with demonstrating his talents and skills and with presenting a finished art-object than with suggesting significance in the occasion.

Given this background, the poem, for all its conceptual thinness and traditional modes and devices, does show a skill well above mere competence. The few awkward rhymes ("tyre" and "wyre", st. 4) and lines ("So let the friendly prickle never digge / Thy watchfull breast with wound or small or bigge," st. 6) are far overweighed by many fine lines, phrases, and stanzas:

Tell me ye velvet violets
That fringe the crooked banke with gawdie blewe,
So let with comely grace your prettie frets
Be spread, so let a thousand *Zephyrs* sue
To kisse your willing heads, that seeme t'eschew
    Their wanton touch with maiden modestie,
    So let the silver dewe but lightly lie
Like little watrie world within your azure skie.

(st. 8)

This stanza perfectly demonstrates the pattern or formula discussed above; it also flawlessly achieves the basic purpose of that formula: to produce lovely, graceful, fluid, musical language in poetic form. It more than bears comparison with many like stanzas of pastoral verse by Sidney, Spenser, Lyly, Peele, Greene, or Drayton. It is, in short, a lovely and graceful piece of verse.

Although Giles' poem is essentially Elizabethan in its qualities (perhaps Spenserian in diction and pointing), some images reflect a new direction, a new emphasis which shortly became an earmark of new styles of writing in a new poetic age: for example, the stream that becomes suds of "frothy creame" (st. 1) to "imitate the whiteness" of Ocyroe, and "The very waters when she sunke did showe / With many wrinckled ohs they sympathiz'd her woe" (st. 11). These quotations reflect the type of graphic metaphor and exaggerated analogy that modern readers associate with John Donne and other Metaphysical poets of the seventeenth century. Like a precursor, Giles' poem points forward to the "monarchy of Wit" which was to rule the literary world of Jacobean and Caroline England.

V "O dearest Prince"

The death of Prince Henry in 1612, like that of Elizabeth earlier, produced poetic response from the university community. *Epicedium Cantabrigiense, In obitum immaturum, semperque deflendum, Henrici, Illustrissimi Principis Walliae* . . . (Cambridge, 1612), a collection of memorial poems in foreign and classical tongues, contained two Latin poems by Giles Fletcher; and the second printing in the same year added a section of English poems, which included another poem by Giles. Such books as *Sorrowes Joy* and *Epicedium Cantabrigiense* represent a small, unheralded, but nevertheless significant poetic tradition in England. For one thing, they carried grammar school and college compositional practice to a higher artistic and professional level. For another, like college and university literary magazines today, they played an important role in the promulgation and advancement of literature. During the Renaissance, most of the literature in them was in Latin; and the body of extant neo-Latin poetry produced at the two universities during the sixteenth and seventeenth centuries is large. Perhaps more important to us today, much of the verse in English that was produced during the period differs from the Latin mainly in language. Many of the best poets of the age—Milton for example—first saw print in these memorial volumes.

Giles' two Latin poems were "In fatum summi, & beatissimi Principis Henrici," an hexameral elegy of fifty-four lines, and "Carmen Sepulchrale," four couplets of elegiac verse. Thomas Fuller in *The Church-History of Britain* (1655) said of the latter, "made by Giles Fletcher of Trinity College in Cambridge on this PRINCES plain grave, because wanting an inscription." He then quoted and translated the last four lines:

> Si sapis, attonitus sacro decede sepulchro,
>   Nec cineri quae sint nomina quaere novo.
> Prudens celavit sculptor; nam quisque rescivit,
>   Protinus in lachrymas solvitur, & moritur.

G.F.T.C.

> If wise, amaz'd depart this holy *Grave;*
> Nor these *New*-ashes, ask what *Names* they have,
> The *Graver* in concealing them was wise.
> For, who so knows, straight melts in tears and dies.

Giles' English poem, however, is more interesting than his Latin ones. It certainly warrants as much attention and discussion as "Eliza," to which it bears an especially provocative relationship.

Upon the most lamented departure of the right hopefull, and blessed Prince Henrie Prince of Wales.[10]

(1)

> The weeping time of Heav'n is now come in,
>   Kindely the season clowdes of sorrowe beares,
> To smile, o let it be a deadly sinne
> And happy hee, his merry looks forswears,
> See heav'n for us is melted into teares:
>   O deerest Prince how many hearts wear knowne
>   To save thy life, that would have lost their owne?

(2)

> When thou thy Countreys griefe, weart once her glory,
> How was this blessed Isle crown'd with delight;
> So long it never knew how to be sorry,
> But anchor'd all her joyes upon thy sight;
> The musique every whear did freely lite:
>   The Sheapheards pip't, and countrey byrds did sing,
>   The water-nymphs came dauncing from their spring.

(3)

It was the mother then of harmeles pleasure
The Queene of beawty all men came to see,
And poore it could not bee, thou weart her treasure,
Onely it was a mittle prowde of thee,
Aye mee, that ever so it might not bee!
   The Garden of the world, whear nothing wanted,
   Another Paradise, that God had planted.

(4)

Her happie fields wear dec'kt with every flowre,
That with her sweetest lookes Peace smil'd to see it:
Delight it selfe betwixt her breasts did bowre,
And oft her rustique Nymphs thy coach would meet,
And strow with flowers the way before thy feete.
   But now those flowers wee woont to strow before thee,
   Dead, in thy grave wee throw them to adore thee.

(5)

Sleepe softly, royall Ghost, in that cold bed,
Let deaths pale chambers give thee easie rest,
Whear all the Princely bones lie buried,
With guilded crowns and long white scepters drest.
Ah, little look't they thou shouldst be their guest!
   What makes the heav'ns proclaime such open warres?
   Wee did not owe thee so soone to the starres.

(6)

And yet our vowes doe not thy starres envie thee,
Bathe thee in joyes, wee in our teares will swim:
Wee doe not unto heav'n, or God denie thee,
Onely the Muses begge this leave of him,
To fill with teares their fountaine to the brim,
   And as thou sett'st emparadis'd above,
   To powre out to thee rivers of their love.

(7)

See how the yeare with thee is stricken dead,
And from her bosome all her flowers hath throwne,
With thee the trees their haires fling from their head,
And all the Sheapheards pipes are deadly blowne,
All musique now, and mirth is hatefull growne:
   Onely *Halcyons* sad lamenting pleases,
   And that Swans dirge, that, as hee sings, deceases.

(8)

Heav'n at thy death deni'd our world his light,
Ne suff'red one pale starre abroad to peepe,
And all about the world the winds have sigh'd,
Nor can the watrie-nymphs (so fast they weepe)
Within their banks their flouds of sorrow keepe.
   Suffer us, in this deluge of distresse,
    Thee, if not to enjoy, at least to blesse.

(9)

Bedded in all the roses of delight
Let thy engladded soule embalmed lie,
Imbrightned into that celestiall light,
Which all Gods saintly Lamps doth glorifie,
Thear boast thy kinred with the Deitie
Whear God his Sonne, and Christ his Brother greet
   thee,
And thy too little glorious Sisters meete thee.

(10)

But ô thou desert Island, that art found
Cast in the seas deepe bosome by mishap,
As if with our salt teares thou all weart drown'd,
And hadst from heav'n drop't into sorrowes lap:
Desolate house! what mantle now shall wrap
   Thy naked sides? poore widow, made to mourne,
    To whom wilt thou thy sad addresses tourne?

(11)

Alas, the silent Angels on his tombe
Can him no honour, thee no comfort sing,
Their pretie weeping lookes may well become
Themselves, but him to life can never bring.
Thee therefore, deerest Prince, from perishing
   Or yet alive wee in our hearts will save,
    Or dead with thee, our hearts shall be thy grave.

(12)

Henrie farewell, heav'ns soone-restored Exile,
Immortall Garland of thy Fathers head,
Mantle of honour to this naked Isle,
Bright drop of heav'n, on whose wish't nuptiall bed
Now all our ripest hopes hung blossomed.
   Farewell, farewell; hearke how the Angels sing,
    On earth our Prince is now in heav'n a King.

                               G. F. T. C.

The poem memorialized Henry by suggesting his importance to England's cultural and emotional life (past, present, and future) as well as to Heaven's scheme of things and its relation to England. A brief "anatomy" of this poem, to use the favorite seventeenth-century term of analysis, reveals some interesting comparisons and contrasts with "A Canto upon . . . Eliza." The external form of the two poems is almost exactly the same: twelve stanzas of rhyme royal (*ababbcc;* however, the earlier poem had an additional line, a final alexandrine). Beyond this comparison, the two poems could hardly be more dissimilar. The internal structure, or skeleton, of "Prince Henrie" follows generally that of the traditional elegy: the first section (st. 1) announces the sad occasion of the poem; section two (sts. 2 - 4) commemorates what Henry had been to England; section three (sts. 5 - 7) deals with present loss and lamentation; section four (sts. 8 - 9) begins the immortalizing; section five (sts. 10 - 12) deals with the paradox of England's seeming loss but ultimate gain from Henry's death. The concluding couplet forms something of a formal epitaph: "Farewell, farewell; heare how the Angels sing, / On earth our Prince is now in heav'n a King."

Other internal unity results from an impressively complex fabric of images, themes, and motifs (perhaps like sinews and muscles, to continue the anatomical analogy): *water* (tears, sea, rivers, fountains, deluge, flood); *music* (shepherd's pipes, birds' singing, Angels' songs); *flowers* (garlands, roses of delight, floral tributes, etc.); *Island* (England); *Paradise* (garden, fields, Heaven); *Mother* (Queen of Beauty, widow, nymphs, Halcyone); as well as *mantle, house, bed* (nuptual and grave), *stars,* and so forth. Still other and different internal structuring appears in the interlacing of stanzas through repetition in the last and the first lines (grief, 1 - 2; nymph / mother, 2 - 3; paradisal states, 3 - 4; grave, 4 - 5; stars, 5 - 6, etc.).

The complexity of the interrelating of so many parts reflects another outstanding feature of the anatomy of "Prince Henrie": it reveals a large and active *brain* at work. This may be the single most distinguishing feature between "Eliza" and "Henrie," as well as the quality that most separates the two different poetical worlds they represent. "Eliza" is essentially poetry of the senses; "Henrie," of the mind. The brain dominates "Henrie"; its presence can be felt through every line. Thought, analysis, and concept replace in that poem the coloration, lushness, and sound effects of "Eliza" and form, therefore, an essentially different poetic texture.

A substantial part of the mental dimension of "Henrie" involves *wit,* that discursive and intellectual quality which the court of King James was just beginning to admire, redefine, and prize in life and literature. Quick-wittedness, the ability to see relationships in seemingly disparate things, verbal ingenuity, cleverness, intellectuality, learning, and humor—these are some of the qualities that comprise Jacobean wit. John Donne may have been "The Monarch of Wit" (according to Thomas Carew), and Ben Jonson and the Cavalier poets may have been the leading courtiers in that "Monarchy," but Giles Fletcher, Jr. demonstrates sharpness of poetic wit in this poem before that "Monarchy" was even recognized.

The conceit is, of course, one of the marks of the wit-poetry of the century. The seedling conceits of "Eliza," previously noted, have become a summer garden in "Henrie." Stanza 10 is indicative:

> But ô thou desert Island, that art found
> Cast in the seas deepe bosome by mishap,
> As if with our salt teares thou all weart drown'd.
> And hadst from heav'n dropt into sorrowes wrap
> Thy naked sides? poore widow, made to mourne,
> To whom wilt thou thy sad addresses tourne?

The first four lines represent a very complex analogy (in an even more complex syntax). The grieving English people become analogous to their own island as well as a star fallen into the sea; and the sea becomes at once a deep bosom, a lap of sorrow, and the people's salt tears. In the next two lines, the analogy rapidly shifts to that of a desolate house, a mantle-draped body, and a mourning widow. In short, the stanza offers not only four to six analogies for the grief of the English people but from four to six *very different* analogies. The poet performs an elaborate piece of artistic gymnastics; as he crosses a high wire, he juggles half a dozen metaphors at once. Most of John Donne's poetry works the same way. "A Valediction: forbidding mourning," for example, offers a dozen analogies for love and separation, including that famous extended conceit of the compass.

Even closer is Donne's poem on the death of his wife, "A Nocturnal on St. Lucies Day," that was written within a few years of "Henrie":

> All others, from all things, draw all that's good,
> Life, soule, forme, spirit, whence they beeing have;
> I, by loves limbecke, am the grave

> Of all, that's nothing. Oft a flood
>   Have wee two wept, and so
> Drownd the whole world, us two; oft did we grow
> To be two Chaosses, when we did show
> Care to ought else; and often absences
> Withdrew our soules, and made us carcasses.

A different type of conceit associated with Donne, the extended as well as exaggerated analogy, forms stanza six of "Henrie":

> And yet our vowes doe not thy starres envie thee,
> Bathe thee in joyes, wee in our teares will swim:
> Wee doe not unto heav'n, or God denie thee,
> Onely the Muses begge this leave of him,
> To fill with teares their fountaine to the brim,
>   And as thou sett'st emparadis'd above,
>   To powre out to thee rivers of their love.

A conceit like Giles Fletcher's in kind and content appears in Richard Crashaw's "The Weeper" (1646) in which the poet describes Mary Magdalene's eyes as,

> Starres indeed they are too true;
> For they but seem to fall,
> As Heavn's other spangles doe.
> It is not for our earth and us
> To shine in Things so pretious.

> Upwards thou dost weep.
> Heavn's bosome drinks the gentle stream.
> Where th' milky rivers creep,
> Thine floates above; and is the cream.
> Waters above th' Heavns, what they be
> We' are taught best by thy TEARES and thee.[11]

The wit in such conceits lies in the intellectual perspicuity or cleverness which can perceive relationships in analogies that are so apparently farfetched. It also resides in ingenuity of language and its manipulation. Certain devices were particularly "witty." Paradox, for example, reverses the thrust of a conceit by stressing contradiction rather than analogy. The poems of Donne and the other Metaphysical poets are not fuller of them than is "Henrie": "And happy hee, his merry looks forswears," (1:4); "To save thy life, that would have lost their owne" (1:7); "Bathe thee in joyes, wee in our teares will swim" (6:2). The convoluted syntax associated with Donnean wit-poetry also characterizes "Henrie":

> Thee therefore, deerest Prince, from perishing
> Or yet alive wee in our hearts will save,
> Or dead with thee, our hearts shall be thy grave

(st. 11)

Inversion of normal word order, as in this passage, also helps account for much of the syntactical obscurity. In fact, inversion is one of the most prominent rhetorical devices in the poem. Hardly a stanza lacks an example or two. This device, plus a good bit of interior punctuation to make the meter irregular, gives a distinct speech rhythm to the poem.

The external similarity in form of "A Canto on the death of Eliza" and "Upon the most lamented departure of . . . Henrie . . . " magnifies the vast internal differences between the two poems. They represent two different poetic styles; they also represent two different literary periods. Literary historians often distinguish the dominant Elizabethan from the Jacobean literary styles through the terms "high Renaissance" and "Baroque" although there are obvious difficulties in applying the same terms to Italian architecture and English poetry. Still, it is possible to relate the features of "Eliza"—the very simple structure, the simple and direct content, the smooth regularity of the verse music, the few but intensely practiced devices for sensuous effect in sound and description—with the "high Renaissance" or the Elizabethan style. It is also possible to relate the conceited, wit-twisted, crabbed, complexly structured, multifaceted and eclectic style of "Henrie" with "Baroque" or Jacobean styles. "Eliza" comes from the world of Sidney, Spenser, Giles, Sr., and the lush, sensuous, richly musical air of Elizabeth's court. "Henrie" speaks from the witty, troubled world of Donne and Jonson, from a world being turned over and reexamined by Bacon (Giles' future patron).[12]

Furthermore, in terms of Giles' own growth as a poet, "Henrie" represents a notable development; for it bears little relationship to Spenser. A fine poem by a mature poet, it has tough, tight verse; it demonstrates economy of language, intense feeling, effective and striking metaphor. It is richly complex in theme, motif, and image—all controlled effectively by Giles. The couplets at the end of each verse are especially strong:

> The Sheapheards pip't, and countrey byrds did sing,
> The water-nymphs came dauncing from their spring.

The final couplet in the fourth stanza also forms a brilliant transition from "happie fields" to deaths pale chambers":

> But now those flowers wee woont to strow before thee,
> Dead, in thy grave wee throw them to adore thee.

The final epithet forms an epigram rivaling those of Ben Jonson:

> Farewell, farewell; hearke how the Angels sing,
> On earth our Prince is now in heav'n a King.

Jonson, however, did not publish his epigrams until four years later. When "Henrie" is considered in conjunction with *Christ's Victorie*, "Henrie" appears very much the work of an innovator who, at the very beginning of a new period, is exhibiting features that will become the identifying characteristics of a great literary age.

CHAPTER 3

Christ's Victorie and Triumph

I *My Whiter Muse*

> my Whiter Muse
> Doth burne in heavenly love, such love to tell,
> O thou that didst this holy fire infuse (*CVT*, I, 3).

GILES Fletcher, Jr.'s complete dedication of life and literature to God is nowhere in his work more strikingly revealed than in *Christ's Victorie and Triumph* (1610). His prefatory "To the Reader," apparently modeled upon Sidney's great "Defense of Poesy," deserves to be more widely known than it is since nowhere in English Renaissance literature appears a more economical or more finely written statement of the claims "for prophane Poetrie to deale with divine and heavenly matters." The opposing, widespread attitude against which Giles' little essay operates is succinctly exemplified in the following statement by one of his contemporaries: "the subject is either *Divine* or *Prophane*. If . . . Divine matter, then are they most intollerable, or rather Sacrilegious."[1]

Also there is no finer example of the new directions and emphasis that Christian Humanism was to take in the seventeenth century. Like Sidney's great "Defense," Giles' statement is presented as a defense of religious poetry in two parts: a history of practice and practitioners, and a philosophic and theoretic consideration of such poetry. Giles concludes with an unforgettable statement: "So beeing nowe weary in perswuading those that hate, I commend my selfe to those that love such Poets, as *Plato* speaks of, that *sing divine and heroical matters* . . . . recommending theas my idle howers, not idly spent, to good schollers, and good Christians, that have overcome their ignorance with reason, and their reason, with religion."[2] For Giles Fletcher, poetry is a perfectly acceptable way to "sing (though I sing sorilie) the love of heaven and earthe, then

41

praise God"; and the praise of God and His works is an equally acceptable subject for poetry ("My Whiter Muse / Doth burne in heavenly love, such love to tell").

Another phrase used by Giles—"enamour'd with this celestial Muse"—completes the picture. He is the first English Renaissance poet publicly to identify himself as *vates* and to dedicate himself seriously to that role. After Giles, many poets in the century included like statements with their work or clearly indicated similar commitment. John Milton (who borrowed considerably from Giles) immediately comes to mind:

These abilities [of poets] are the inspired gift of God rarely bestowed, but yet to some (though most abuse) in every nation; and are of power beside the office of a pulpit, to inbreed and cherish in a great people the seeds of virtue and public civility, to allay the perturbations of the mind and set the affections in right tune, to celebrate in glorious and lofty hymns the throne and equipage of God's almightiness, and what he works and what he suffers to be wrought with high providence in his church, to sing the victorious agonies of martyrs and saints, the deeds and triumphs of just and pious nations doing valiantly through faith against the enemies of Christ. . . . (*The Reason of Church Government*, Bk. II).[3]

Renaissance idealism about poetry, best expressed in England by Sidney, found a thoroughly religious commitment in the seventeenth century. To make that commitment, the Gordian knot of Court-and-Poetry seemingly had to be severed; but no sixteenth-century poets could or would do it. Spenser included religious material in his work (some eclogues of the *Shepherd's Calendar* and in the *Faerie Queene*, for example) but he did so either allegorically or mixed with secular material (as in the *Four Hymns*). Sidney represented the ideal Elizabethan poet, who was secular. Spenser was distinctly moral and religious, but the secular foundation of his work is too obvious. Also, he neither indentified himself as religious poet nor suggested the role of *vates* for himself.

Those poets of the seventeenth century who identified themselves with the role were either intentionally separated from the court or clergymen (or both): for example, Giles and Phineas Fletcher, John Milton, George Herbert, Richard Crashaw to some extent, and John Bunyan. During the century poets began to divide their work into "sacred" and "secular" (Robert Herrick, Thomas Traherne, Richard Crashaw, Henry Vaughan, John Donne, Ben Jonson, and so forth). This practice also reflects the religious-political polarizations that were transpiring at the time.[4]

The theoretic side of Giles' defense follows Sidney's; it argues on the basis of Aristotle, Horace, and Plato that "Poetry" forms a more lofty and effective education than philosophy, history, music, and so forth. Writers cited by Giles include David and the other sacred poets of Scripfure, Nazianzen, Basil, Juvencus, Prosper, Prudentius, Sedulius, Nonnius, Sanazaro, Du Bartas, Spenser, and King James. Giles also mentions genres: "divine Poems of the Genealogie, Miracles, Parables, Passion of Christ" as well as "hymnes, and Psalmes, and spirituall songs." He describes, in short, a variety of forms of religious literature and sixteen or more centuries of practice.

Of particular note are Giles' remarks about Sanazaro, Du Bartas, and Spenser: "*Sanazar*, the late-living Image, and happy imitator of *Virgil*, bestowing ten yeares upon a song, onely to celebrat that one day when Christ was borne unto us on earth, & we (a happie change) unto God in heav'n: thrice-honour'd *Bartas*, & our (I know no other name more glorious then his own) Mr. Edmund Spencer (two blessed Soules). . . ." Giles' debt to these three (and Vergil makes four) appears notable in *Christ's Victorie and Triumph* and suggests distinct approaches to the poem.

II *Sing Divine and Heroical Matters*

The "divine and heroical matters" about which Giles writes are indicated first in the poem's full title—*Christ's Victorie, and Triumph in Heaven, and Earth, over, and after death*—and then appear in more detail in the opening announcement of the epic subject:

> The birth of him that no beginning knewe,
> Yet gives beginning to all that are borne,
> And how the Infinite farre greater grewe,
> By growing lesse, and how the rising Morne,
> That shot from Heav'n, did backe to heaven retourne,
>   The obsequies of him that could not die,
>   And death of life, ende of eternitie,
> How worthily he died, that died unworthily;
>
> How God, and Man did both embrace each other,
> Met in one person, heav'n, and earth did kiss,
> And how a Virgin did become a Mother,
> And bare that Sonne, who the worlds Father is,
> And Maker of his mother, and how Bliss

Descended from the bosom of the High,
To cloathe himselfe in naked miserie,
Sayling at length to Heav'n, in earth, triumphantly,
Is the first flame, wherewith my whiter Muse
Doth burne in heavenly love, such love to tell.

This passage is glossed with a marginal note: "The Argument propounded in generall: Our Redemption by Christ."

Many modern readers, however, surely must be puzzled by Giles' treatment of his subject, as well as by the general structure of the work. The two main parts of the poem, the "Victory" and the "Triumph" of Christ, are composed of two books each so that the whole poem is comprised of four books: "Christ's Victorie in Heaven" presents a debate between Mercy and Justice and ends with a brief description of Christ's Birth; "Christ's Victorie on Earth" deals with the Temptation of Christ by Satan in the Wilderness; "Christ's Triumph over Death" treats the crucifixion; "Christ's Triumph after Death" presents the Resurrection and Ascension.

Modern readers might see the relationship of "Our Redemption by Christ" to Crucifixion and Resurrection more readily than to Birth and Temptation. They might also wonder why a narrative poem about Christ should contain so few details of Christ's life and ministry and yet so much seemingly extraneous material: for example, allegorical discussions in heaven about Adam and Eve's fall in Eden, wars of angels, Satan's apostasy in heaven, his evil seduction of man in the garden, the creation of the cosmos, the nature of the physical universe, a lengthy description of the heavenly city of God, and multiple allusions to Greek and Latin mythological personages.

Furthermore, the reason Fletcher did not simply present an exciting, straightforward narrative—a genuine life of Christ—in the poem's twenty-two hundred lines may not be at all clear to most readers. However, familiarity with John Milton's *Paradise Lost*, *Paradise Regained*, and "On the Morning of Christ's Nativity" would be helpful, since the relationship between the two poets is more extensive than the fact that Milton borrowed from Giles' poem, or that his "Christ's Nativity" bears close relation to the nativity descriptions in *Christ's Victorie and Triumph* (Bk. I), or that *Paradise Regained* is even closer to Book II of *Christ's Victorie and Triumph*. More important, *Paradise Lost* and *Christ's Victorie and Triumph* are two literary versions of the same story; they are products of the same literary tradition and are even jointly influenced by many of the same writers and works. Since this tradition has been largely lost to us, and since it affects so many writers as well as relates otherwise disparate works of the period, especially those of the Fletchers, some discussion appears necessary.

The story of Lucifer's apostasy in heaven, the fall of the apostate angels to hell, the creation of the world, Satan's temptation of Man in the garden, Man's fall, Christ's redemptive mission, and diverse events of subsequent history to the Last Judgment had been given literary form many hundreds of times in different languages, genres, and degrees of completeness between early Christian times and the seventeenth century. The story developed primarily in the Hebrew-Christian world about 200 B.C. to 200 A.D. Some evidence of its growth appears in the New Testament, but this story largely postdates the Scripture, and, as a whole, appears nowhere in Scripture. This body of material from Hebrew-Christian mythology slowly coalesced into a recognizable story. Modern commentators have described it variously as the orthodox scheme from Creation to Last Judgment, the story of the Fall of Man, the celestial cycle, the genesis tradition, and so forth.[5]

The story grew with Christianity as an addendum to Scripture and spread with it throughout the world. It became an integral, fundamental part of the Christian world-view for at least ten to fifteen centuries; and it was manifoldly enmeshed with numerous, basic Christian dogmas and beliefs (Original Sin, Satan, Providence, Christ's Redemptive Mission, Salvation, and many more). The efficacy and influence of the story reached a climax during the Renaissance. By the beginning of the eighteenth century, the story and the whole tradition involving mythological Christianity, of which it was a part, were in rapid decline as the result of the influence of science and rationalism on religion and theology.

The story is simple in narrative components but complex and multifarious in significant ramifications. Like the Hebrew-Christian providential view of history of which it is an outgrowth, the story was a semimythological, fabled version of history that also formed a framework of history. An ontological, teleological, and eschatological myth framed by the alpha and omega of divine history (the Creation and Last Judgment), it provided, among other things, a narrative framework for the well-known cosmic drama of God, Man, and Satan.

Its literary value—not to mention its theological and homiletic—was considerable. For over seventeen centuries, the story was used as a framework (as well as subject and material) for myriad literary and quasi-literary works. Lucifer's Apostasy and Fall, Man's Creation and Fall, Christ's redemptive mission, and the Last Judgment were core events. A wide variety of scriptural episodes (and post-scriptual history) were regularly incorporated within the all-encompassing framework. The story offered almost unlimited possibilities for literary development, concentration, arrangement, and selection, as a staggeringly diversified body of extant works demonstrates. The extreme flexibility and adaptability of the story are evidenced also by the fact that it appears in almost every known genre and conceivable length, from the 287 lines of Spenser's "A Hymn of Heavenly Love" to the 250 pages of Bunyan's allegorical *The Holy War* or to the twelve books of Milton's epic, *Paradise Lost.*

But perhaps the most pertinent fact in terms of Giles Fletcher's version in *Christ's Victorie and Triumph* is that many writers used the story skeletally as the background and framework for concentrated treatment of single events from it: the war in heaven, the temptation and fall, or the Nativity, for example. Sanazaro's *De Partu Virginis* (which Giles specifically mentions in "To the Reader"), Prudentius' "Kalendas Ianuarius," and Milton's "On the morning of Christ's Nativity" all celebrate Christ's birth in terms of the larger story of Christian history and providence, just as Giles does in Book I of *Christ's Victorie and Triumph;* and Milton deals the same way with the temptation of Christ in *Paradise Regained.*

The writers specifically mentioned by Giles in "To the Reader" indicate even more clearly the tradition from which *Christ's Victorie* emanates. Du Bartas' main works, *Divine Weeks,* translated into English in 1608 by J. Sylvester, was probably the most influential literary work of its time, as well as a version of the Christian story of divine history. The six days of creation form the structure for this huge allegorical epic (23,000 lines). Prudentius' *Psychomachia* presents the struggle of good and evil as an epic war; his *Hamartigenia* deals with episodes of scriptural history. Sedulius' *Carmen Paschale* is a version of the story in five books; Spenser's "A Hymn of Heavenly Love," a version in 1,753 lines.

Viewed against this background, *Christ's Victorie and Triumph* takes on a special unity which a modern reader might miss. This unity connects such otherwise disparate works as those mentioned above with countless other versions of the story. Such simple narrative unity has behind it the profound significance of the whole mythological Christian tradition, whose roots were implanted deep in the soil of Christian beliefs for many centuries.

In short, *Christ's Victorie and Triumph* is a version of the Christian story of divine history; and Giles' poem centers structurally on four episodes from Christ's life: Nativity, Temptation, Passion, and Resurrection. Each of these is celebrated as a victory; each forms the center of one book; and each is part of the great Victory of Christ over Satan, Sin, and Death. Around each is woven a vast panoply of Christian history and beliefs. Unlike most versions, Giles' poem is distinctly Christocentric. It could be viewed, therefore, as the first English *Christiad* (Vida's famous *Christiados*, a Latin epic in six books, appeared in 1527); and it is surely the most unusual.

III *Résumé, Book I*

The first book, "Christ's Victorie in Heaven" (85 stanzas), begins with the announcement of the subject of the whole poem and then invokes Giles' "Whiter Muse" that "didst this holy fire infuse / And taught'st this brest" the love and knowledge of God. Invoking the Holy Spirit instead of a classical Muse not only represents an innovation in the Christian Humanist literature of the English Renaissance but also prepares the reader for another innovation, the direct treatment of religious subjects.[6] The action begins in heaven amidst saints and angels with a debate between Justice and Mercy (personified) over fallen Man:

> Could Justice be of sinne so over-wooed,
> Or so great ill be cause of so great good,
> That bloody man to save, mans Saviour shed his blood?
>
> O say, say how could Mercie plead for those
> That scarcely made, against their Maker rose? (4 - 5)

Mercy pleads for guilty man with "the musique of her voice" (7 - 9). Justice "not deafe and blind," but "a Virgin of austere regard," carrying a sword and amidst a retinue of allegorical personages, is described in the style and manner of late Medieval, early Renaissance (especially Spenserian) poetry (10 - 14):

> The winged Lightning is her Mercury,
> And round about her mightie thunders sound:
> Impatient of himselfe lies pining by
> Pale Sickness, with his kercher'd head upwound,
> And thousands noysome plagues attend her round,
>   But if her clowdie browe but once growe foule,
>   The flints doe melt, and rocks to water rowle,
> And ayrie mountaines shake, and frighted shadowes howle (12).

Justice then addresses a long speech to "All heav'n," a speech, over twenty-two stanzas long (17 - 39) that forms a major subdivision of Book I. "Her accusation of Man's sinne" presents a good deal of the story of divine history; for, beginning with Adam and Eve, she traces their descendants in terms primarily of their idolatry of Satan and of the pagan deities and oracles (18 - 24). This recital is followed by an indictment of "wicked, unjust, impure man" (25 - 27) that relates how man has become separated from other creatures and from his physical surroundings (28 - 33), how he is ungrateful to God (34 - 5), and how hopeless and remediless his situation has become (35 - 9). Justice calls for punishment: "Death to dead men, justice to unjust." Hearing the speech, the heavenly Hierarchies and the Almighty "Flam'd all in just revenge, and mightie thunder" (40).

Mercy then arises, is described, and defends man. Christ is discussed and his Nativity described. This section, which forms the remainder of the book (41 - 83), except for two concluding stanzas, divides neatly into two main parts: the description of Mercy (41 -69) and her speech (70 - 83). Mercy's manifold beauties are described first (41 - 6); second, her attendants, her persuasive powers, kind offices to man (47 - 52); and third, her garment, which depicts and symbolizes the created universe (53 - 63). Mercy's speech (70 - 83) defends Man by imputing the main fault to Satan, by asking why the Devil has not been sentenced to die, and by pleading "mercy" due to Man's inferiority to heavenly Spirits (70 -4). She calls attention to the Son of God, Christ, who is below on earth and who represents a solution that is both just and merciful:

> What hath man done, that man shall not undoe,
> Since God to him is grown so neere a kin?
> Did his foe slay him? He shall slay his foe:
> Hath he lost all? he all againe shall win;
> Is sinne his Master? He shall master sinne:

> Too hardy soule, with sinne the field to trie:
> The onely way to conquer was to flie,
> But thus long death hath liv'd, and now deathe
> selfe shall die (76).

This passage leads to the climax of Book I, the narration and celebration of Christ's Nativity: "The Time . . . when . . . God himself now like a mortall man became" (78). The birth of Him "That with one hand the vaults of heav'n could shake (as in Milton's later Nativity poem) is described in terms of its effects upon the world; and among these are a blow to the Forces of Satan ("The cursed Oracles wear strucken dumb," 82), establishment of a new King on Earth (Christ), Peace, and Proclamation of the "Saviour to posteritie." The Nativity, or Christ's first victory, that is described appropriately in heaven where it was conceived, is symbolized by the response in heaven to Mercy's speech. God, the Father, and the Angelic armies disavow "Their former rage, and all to Mercie b[ow'd]" (84).

IV *Commentary on Book I*

Book I is static rather than dramatic. The art, mirrored in the structure and in the technique, produces a sense of timeless significance—one of emblematic celebration rather than of drama or action. The first book focuses attention upon themes and qualities rather than upon events and characters and the central technical device used by Giles is the "figure." The efficacy of the "figure," although considerable for Giles' contemporaries, is almost totally lost on the literate reader of today since the whole tradition passed away with the twofold demise of formal education based upon Christian Humanism (that Renaissance blend of Classicism and formal religious education) and of the widespread use of allegory. A "figure" during the Renaissance was, to oversimplify, an allegorical character with definite literary reputation and associations. Through repeated usage in diverse contexts, a "figure" was closer than other allegorical personifications to a symbol; it was rich and multifarious in meaning rather than singular. Since Justice and especially Mercy are such "figures" (Sapience, in "A Hymn of Heavenly Beauty," may have suggested Mercy), they would bring to the poem for the Renaissance reader something of the stature and dimension of a celebrity.

Mercy, who actually dominates Book I, is a "figure" rich in meanings. Giles, who calls her a "faire Idea" (43:3; 63:1), can not describe her because she is a platonic Ideal: an Absolute, the perfect Idea of mercy, she is existent only in the mind of God; all known instances of mercy (merciful acts, etc.) are but imperfect versions of that Ideal. Her beauties must be described by analogy to physical things, for she exists on the same level as Beauty, Truth, Reason, and like abstractions. Her garments, which depict the whole Created Cosmos (heaven and earth), symbolize her closeness to the Creator and her permeation of the Created Universe. Like Love, Justice, Wisdom, and Faith, she represents a segment of the mind of God, but she also represents the Son. In short, Mercy operates in many capacities in the poem: she is a character, an act, a theme, a value, a quality, a theological principle, a mystery of Faith, an Ideal, a symbol.

The art of Book I is the art of the emblem, of figure, of allegory rather than the art of representation, realism, story, and character. Description and rhetorical embellishments are important features of its esthetic. However, except in a few instances like the allegorical retinue of Justice, the first book sounds and reads quite unlike works from the Middle Ages and from the early Renaissance which employ a comparable art; and the reasons are discussed in the next chapter.

V Résumé, Book II

The second victory, "Christ's Victorie on Earth," is the Son's overcoming of Satan's temptations in the wilderness. The three Gospel accounts in Matthew 4, Mark 1, and Luke 4 jointly provided at best a paragraph of details and perhaps a rough outline of sorts. Giles' poem, which is sixty-two stanzas and over five hundred lines long, begins with the non-scriptural action of Mercy and her Graces when they descend from heaven to "a poor Desolate," Christ in the wilderness ("the place of comfort"); when they enter "his brest" (1 - 2), Mercy becomes part of Christ, completes a transition from Book I to II, and disappears from the poem as a separate personage. Christ is recognized and adored by the animals as their Lord (3 - 6), and his Godhead in man and nature is described (6 - 7). His beauty is described at length in very sensuous terms, with biblical allusions and with epic similes (8 - 14).

Satan, disguised as a devoted "old Hermit" and reciting prayers, humbly greets Christ and invites him to his underground cell (15 -

19). On the way, he tempts Christ "to despaire of Gods providence and provide for himself" by turning stones to bread (20 - 23). They arrive at "that infernal cave," a "balefull bowre," in which dwells the allegorical personification DESPAIRE. The cave—"Darke, dolefull, dreary . . . for carrion carkasses" and Despaire herself—are described at length (24 - 9). There, Satan as the Serpent, "woo'd him [Christ] with his charmes . . . to entangle him in sinne," but is recognized and resisted by the Son (29 - 30). Satan then takes Christ to the pinnacle of a temple where another allegorical personage, PRESUMPTION, has a "pavillion" peopled by "lewd throng" in a "fooles paradise" (32 - 6). She tempts Christ to show whether he be "sonne of God or no" by casting himself to the ground (37).

He declines, she falls instead (38), and he is then taken to a hilltop garden and the court of PANGLORIE with its "bowre of Vaine-Delight" (39ff). This pleasure garden of the senses is presented in great length and detail (39 - 59). Noteworthy are the descriptions of other paradisiac gardens; the floral lushness; the artificially rich fountains and streams; the "wild Orgialls" of drink and lust; the upper room of Avarice, "Whear mounts of gold, and flouds of silver run"; the room above Avarice of "Ambition," where "chairs of State" and "diadems" for kingdoms wait; and, above it all, "Panglories blazing throne," from which the "sorceresse" sings a "wooing song" to Christ.

That song, forty-six lines of tetrameter couplets, forms the climax of this temptation and of Book II. If Christ will "Onely bend thy knee to mee, / Thy wooing shall thy winning bee"; for Panglorie offers all pleasures, wealth, and kingdoms as well as her love:

> But he her charmes dispersed into winde,
> And her of insolence admonished,
> And all her optique glasses shattered.
> So with her Syre to hell shee took her flight (60).

Thereupon, Christ's victory over Satan is sung by all nature and by the "holy quires" of Angels. He is fed and headed home victorious (61 - 2).

VI *Commentary, Book II*

The second book differs from the first in several ways. First, it is much more of a straightforward narrative; second, it deals with its principal event, the Temptation of Christ, directly and exclusively (rather than indirectly and inclusively as in Book I). Readers familiar with how scanty and varied are the accounts of the episode in the Gospels will be reminded again what an important tradition of interpretation had accrued over the centuries through biblical exegesis, commentary, and homiletic enlargement. However, modern Christians may still find it difficult to place as much importance on Christ's temptation in the wilderness as upon his Passion and Crucifixion. But Giles was not alone either in theological or literary emphasis among his contemporaries. The idea that Christ, as second Adam, had demonstrated that man could overcome the temptations of Satan was a popular one in the Renaissance.

The age was passionately concerned with trial and temptation; the Calvinists were particularly so; and the literature reflects this concern. Trial and temptation are central concerns in Spenser's *Faerie Queene* and in most of Milton's prose and poetry (*Paradise Lost, Paradise Regained*, and *Samson Agonistes* especially). Milton equated the regaining of paradise with Christ's victory in the wilderness rather than at Calvary. That view may be excessive for the age, but Milton's unforgettable words in *Aereopagitica* are not: "I can not praise a fugitive and cloistered virtue, unexercised and unbreathed, that never sallies out and sees her adversary, but slinks out of the race where that immortal garland is to be run for, not without dust and heat. Assuredly we bring not innocence into the world, we bring impurity much rather: that which purifies us is trial, and trial is by what is contrary." Milton concludes that paragraph with a comment which applies directly to Book II of Giles' poem: "which was the reason why our sage and serious poet Spenser, whom I dare be known to think a better teacher than Scotus or Aquinas, describing true temperance under the person of Guyon, brings him in with his palmer through the cave of Mammon and the bower of earthly bliss, that he might see and know, and yet abstain."[7]

The passage in Spenser's *Faerie Queene* (Bk. II) to which Milton refers is almost surely the source of Giles' Cave of Despaire and Bower of Vaine Delight. In fact, Giles' Book II, "Christ's Victorie on Earth," reminds us of Spenser's *Faerie Queene* in almost every way: episodes, use and type of allegory, action, place, style, verse texture, and the pace of the narrative. Both poems rely heavily upon description and not at all upon characterization or drama. Milton knew both poems; his *Paradise Regained* differs from both yet seems also to have been colored by each. For critics who see Giles Fletcher as a literary bridge from Spenser to Milton, "Christ's Victorie on Earth" (Bk. II) provides excellent evidence.

VII *Résumé, Book III,*
"Christ's Triumph Over and After Death"

Book III, "Christ's Triumph Over Death," deals with the Passion and Crucifixion, and celebrates more than narrates these events. The poet's own voice dominates the poem just as a priest's dominates the liturgy. Details and themes from the Scripture concerning the Passion are used more like motifs in liturgy than as the events of a narrative. The structure of the poem also, as evidenced by Giles' marginal glosses, appears rational and discursive like tract or sermon rather than episodic as in narrative. In fact, these glosses form an outline which has been numbered and filled out to provide a description and to demonstrate the structure:

I. "Christs Triumph over death, on the crosse, exprest in generall"

 A. "by his joy to undergoe it: singing before he went to the garden, Mat. 26. 30." Christ as "Triumphant Swan," like Apollo singing "his dirge" on the river Eridan, represents a true Christian Humanist's fusion of classical and Christian elements (1). Christ as singer of heavenly music, and what it means to the poet, follows (2 - 3).

 B. [The Triumph expressed] "By his griefe in the undergoing it." Christ's suffering and its meaning to the poet (and Christians) is recited (4 - 6), especially with imagery of rivers and water.

 C. [The Triumph expressed] "By the obscure fables of the Gentiles typing it." Classical myths and figures are shown to be types (typology) of Old Testament figures, who foreshadow Christ: Deucalion—Noah's flood, Nisus—Sampson, Phaethon—all men, Orpheus—Christ (7 - 8).

 D. [The Triumph expressed] "By the effect it should have in us" (general moralizing with reference to Adam and Eden, 10 - 12).

 E. [The Triumph expressed] "By the instrument of the cursed Tree." The idea of Christ as a second Adam, strong in Book II, is further developed in reference to the Cross as the second tree from which man ate the forbidden fruit in Eden

54

and the paradox of the fortunate fall: "Ah, cursed tree, and yet O blessed fruit!" (13).

II. Christ's Triumph over Death, on the cross, "exprest in particular."

    A. "By his fore-passion in the Garden." A long section (14 - 25) develops the parallel of Eden and Gethsemane: "Sweete Eden was the arbor of delight, / Yet in his hony flo[w'r]s our poyson blew; / Sad Gethseman the bowre of balefull night, / Whear Christ a health of poison for us drewe" (14). Not only is the Christian story of divine history being presented in an unusual way, but also in terms of the paradoxes of the Christian faith as well as its struggle with Satan, the adversary:

> A Man was first the author of our fall,
> A Man is now the author of our rise,
> A Garden was the place we perisht all,
> A Garden is the place he payes our price,
> And the old Serpent with a newe devise (15).

> So the darke Prince, from his infernall cell,
> Casts up his griesly Torturers of hell
> And whets them to revenge . . . (19)

    B. "By his passion itself, amplified. . . ."

        (1) "from the general causes." Described are Peter drowsing and Judas the betrayer awake (26); this becomes extended moralizing on "Betrayal" (27), on human frailty (28 - 9), and on the effects: "Our night is day, our sicknes health is growne," etc. (29).

        (2) "From the particular causes." Details from the scriptural accounts of the Passion—night, the betrayal, the judges, the journey to Calvary, the crucifixion—are woven into a poetic, rhetorical texture which moralizes on human frailty, various sins, and their effects in heaven, on earth, and among the Jews (30 - 9). A long, lurid section is devoted to the effects on Judas (40 - 52): his relationship with Satan, his suicide, his soul tortured in hell with fire and fiends are described with all the zeal and gusto of Michael Wigglesworth in *Doomsday*. The effect, "In the blessed Joseph, &c." takes the form of a long speech of lamentation to Mary by Joseph, "The Arimathean

Swaine" (52 - 64). Mary is presented as a weeping
"Philomel" (65 - 7, completing the classical-Christian
fusion with which the poem opened). The ending of the
poem is focused upon her: "and all about her plaintive
notes she flings, / And their untimely fate most pittifully
sings."

VIII   *Commentary, Book III*

The third book differs from the first two in interesting ways.
Aside from the rational, sermonlike structure and the near absence
of narrative movement in Book III, there are neither allegories nor
figures. Few readers find anything very Spenserian about this section of the work; even description seems minimal. Because evocaton
and expatiation further the liturgical quality, the reader in effect
follows a series of sermonlike, poetic effusions of a religious-moral-
ethical nature over known aspects of the Passion. Since the Passion
itself is not described, the reader has no chance to respond in-
dependently to it; he can only respond to the poet's response to the
Passion. As in the mass or public worship, the stimuli and responses
are both written in and articulated. Book III is liturgical and
devotional, therefore, rather than meditative or narrational in its
methods, ends, and art.
   In this sense, Book III is a celebration, and a public one, of the
Passion as a Triumph. It is more concerned with the significance
and meaning of the Passion than with Christ's experience of it. All
the devices of the art of rhetoric work toward a public goal, and the
voice which carries the reader is that of the *vates* (literally as well as
figuratively). The introductory and concluding framework of
classical analogy, only a few stanzas thick at each end, underscore
"literary" without eschewing "liturgical."

IX   *Résumé, Book IV*
"Christ's Triumph after Death"

Book IV, a continuation of Book III in almost every way, has
perhaps even less narrative and a more celebrational thrust. The
fourth book has the same type of rational, sermonlike structure as
Book III, as reflected in the marginal glosses, which again have
been arranged in outline:
   I.   "Christ's Triumph after death. In his Resurection,
        manifested"

A.   "by the effects of it in the Creatures." Relying heavily
     upon animism and pathetic fallacy, an impressive awaken-
     ing of the physical universe and nature is evoked as sym-
     bolic of Christ's resurrection (1 - 10): "Morning" awakes
     from her bower in the East (1); and the sun awakes spring
     flowers (2 - 3), mountains (4), Earth (5), then trees, birds,
     flowers, and so forth.

B.   "In himself." Stanzas 10 - 13 form a transition from
     nature to Him "Whose garment was before indipt in
     blood, / But now, inbright'ned into heav'nly flame."

II. Christ's Triumph "In his ascension to heaven, whose joyes are
     described" (13 - 15).

     A.   "By the access of all good, the blessed Societie of the
          Saints, Angels, &c." (17 - 19).

          (1) "The sweete quiet and peace under God" (20).

          (2) "Shadowed by the peace we enjoy under our
               Soveraigne." This section (21 - 26) compares
               England's peace to Europe's strife, then moves to
               direct and hyperbolic address to the Monarch in what
               seems like an appeal for royal recognition or favor.

          (3) "The beauty of the place" (27).

          (4) "The c[l]arite (as the schoole cals it) of the Saints
               bodies." This describes the transformation of the
               Faithful and Saints with God's ascension (28 - 31).

          (5) "The impletion of the Appetite" (32 - 3, effect of be-
               ing with God).

          (6) "The joy of the senses, &c." (34, as means of describ-
               ing the joys of being with God in heaven).

     B.   "By the amotion of all evill" (35 - 7, life with evil gone).

     C.   "By the accesse of all good againe in the glorie of the Holy
          Cittie." A description of the City of God in terms of
          precious jewels follows Revelations and the Medieval
          tradition (37 - 8).

          (1) "In the beatificall vision of God." Four stanzas
               describe "th' Idea Beatificall: / End, and beginning of
               each thing that growes / Whose selfe no end, nor yet
               beginning knowes." This description is at once of God
               and the beatific vision of heavenly life eternal (39 -
               42).

          (2) "And of Christ." Five stanzas (43 - 48) extend the
               beatific vision to Christ, "As in his burning throne he

sits emparadis'd." The rather exalted description turns
upon the figures of Christ as Prince, Shepherd, and
Music:

Among those white flocks, and celestiall traines,
  That feed upon Sheapheards eyes, and frame
  That heav'nly musique of so woondrous fame,
Psalming aloude the holy honours of his name (43).

Book IV ends in a final burst of love poetry with the
Church and Christ as mystical lovers and spouses: "His
deerest Spouse, Spouse of the deerest Lover."

III. Conclusion (49 - 51): The last three stanzas evoke brother
Phineas ("Young Thyrsilus," Phineas' pastoral pseudonym)
whose poetic Muse of pastorals, hymns, and love poetry is
contrasted with Giles' "Green Muse," that "Dares not those
high amours, and love-sick songs assay." The poem concludes
with the difficulty of doing justice to the subject:

Impotent words, weake sides, that strive in vaine,
In vaine, alas, to tell so heav'nly sight,
So heav'nly sight, as none can greater feigne,
Feigne what he can, that seems of greatest might,
  Might any yet compare with Infinite?
  Infinite sure those joyes, my word but light,
Light is the pallace whear she swells. O blessed wight!

X *Commentary, Book IV*

The final stanza, with its highly stylized and rhetorical features,
forms an ideal introduction for a critical analysis of the entire poem.
Book IV, which is an extension in most ways of Book III, builds
gradually toward a thematic and rhetorical rather than an emotional
climax in the "Beatific Vision." It underscores how important in
Fletcher's art and style is thematic richness and its development;
and how eclectic, emblematic, and nonnarrative is the essential texture. That Milton should have found guidance in this book surprises
no one who has read both poets.

CHAPTER 4

Christ's Victorie and Triumph, II

I *Style*

IN describing the persuasive powers of Mercy (I,48), Giles
Fletcher could well be describing the very basis of his own poetic
art:

> As melting hony, dropping from the combe,
> So still the words, that spring between thy lipps,
> Thy lippes, whear smiling sweetnesse keepes her home,
> And heav'nly Eloquence pure manna sipps,
> He that his pen but in that fountaine dipps,
>   How nimbly will the golden phrases flie,
>   And shed forth streames of choycest rhetorie
> Welling celestiall torrents out of poesie? (I,48)

Indeed, "the golden phrases flie . . . streames of choycest
rhetorie, / Welling celestiall torrents out of poesie." In an age of
great stylists, the author of *Christ's Victorie and Triumph*
demonstrates one of the most self-conscious and rhetorical of styles.
The elaborate anadiplosis (the repetition of last and first words in
succeeding lines) with which the poem ends exemplifies but the
final drop from those "streames of choycest rhetorie." Every stanza
of the poem offers almost perfect examples of the hundreds of
rhetorical figures and devices which filled rhetoric textbooks. A
review of the major ones used by Giles (and Phineas) serves jointly
to describe some of the particulars of the style and to remind the
reader of a great but at present nearly defunct art.[1]

As with the grand or ciceronian style of prose in the Renaissance,
parallelism in construction is one of the most notable qualities of
Giles' style. The three large devices for achieving balanced phrasing
and construction—isocolon, parison, and paromoion (succeeding
clauses and phrases of equal length, equal structure, and like sound

effects)—all appear regularly. Sometimes the parallelism is a form
of simple repetition:

> One touch would rouze me from my sluggish hearse,
> One word would call me to my wished home,
> One looke would polish my afflicted verse
> One thought would steale my soule from her
> thicke lome. (I, 44)

At other times, the construction is much more complex and
elaborate. In the following example, ellipsis (dropping an important
grammatical part of speech), rhetorical question, and repetition
form significant aspects of the isocolon, parison, and paromoion:

> His strength? but dust: his pleasure? cause of paine:
> His hope? False courtier: youth, or beawtie? brittle:
> Intreatie? fond: repentance? late, and vaine:
> Just recompence? the world wear all too little:
> Thy love? he hath no title to a tittle:
> Hells force? in vaine her furies hell shall gather?
> His Servants, Kinsmen, or his children rather?
> His child, if good, shall judge, if bad, shall
> curse his father. (I, 36)

A different but simpler pattern of reversal also appears:

> He is a path, if any be misled,
> He is a robe, if any naked bee,
> If any chaunce to hunger, he is bread,
> If any be a bondman, he is free. (I, 77)

Antithesis is another recurrent device of parallelism:

> I looke for glorie, but find miserie;
> I looke for joy, but finde a sea of teares;
> I looke that we should live, and finde him die;
> I looke for Angels songs, and heare him crie. (III, 4)

One finds variations of these patterns on every page for Giles relies
very heavily upon devices of parallelism and balanced construction.

Along with these, a multitude of other rhetorical figures and
devices, "flowers" as they were called, appear. Oxymorons, which
seem to be a favorite device of Giles, are often alliterative: "restless

rest" (II, 38, 6); "freezing fire" (I, 25, 2). Word plays and puns occur as regularly as in Shakespeare: "no title to a tittle" (I, 36, 5;
alliteration also figures in these); "The swelling sea seethes" (I, 29,
1); "the dust . . . above the industrious skie" (I, 4, 4); "And him to
prey, as he to pray began" (II, 1, 6). The sound-alike puns,
paronomasia, are particularly prevalent: "his roofe, and arbour har-
bour was," (II, 14, 6); "Maker of the man, or manner of his
making" (I, 73, 8). Antimetabole (repetition of words or ideas in inverse order) and antimetathesis (inversion of the members of an antithesis) appear:

> Or so great ill be cause of so great good,
> That bloody man to save, mans Saviour shed his blood. . . .
>   (I, 4, 7 - 8)
> Mans Murderer to save, mans Saviour to slaie . . .
>   (III, 30, 8)
> To goe to helpe, that must be help't to goe. . . .
>   (I, 37, 5)
> So faire thou art that all would thee behold
> But none can thee behold, thou art so faire. . . .
>   (I, 52, 1 - 2)

In addition, one can find examples of epanadiplosis, epanalepsis,
epanapho4a (or anaphora), epanastrophe, epanodos, epanorthosis
(devices of word and phrase repetition), or a hundred other such
devices from the pages of Thomas Wilson's *The Arte of Rhetorique*
(1553) or other major school texts.

A number of the "flowers" of rhetoric involve sound effects; and
these patterns of sounds formulate the musicality of language.
Paromoion (like sound effects in succeeding clauses and phrases)
figures significantly. Rhyme is, of course, constant in the poem, and
it occurs within lines as well as on the ends: "whom rest doth
flie, / That on salt billowes doth, as pilowes, sleeping lie" (I, 24, 7 -
8). Alliteration, assonance, and consonance appear everywhere (as
in the last example): "clodded in clay," "Lordly lion," "measur'd
many a . . . mile," "lowted low"; and in every conceivable combination.

Another important device for achieving varied sound effects
which plays a notable part in Giles' metrics is the varying of pauses,
or caesura. The following stanza exemplifies an impressive level of
artistry in its structural patterns of caesura:

Who ever sawe Honour before asham'd;	pattern 1
Afflicted Majestie, debased height;	pattern 2
Innocence guiltie, Honestie defam'd;	pattern 2
Libertie bound, Health sick, the Sunne in night?	pattern 3
But since such wrong was offred unto right,	pattern 1
Our night is day, our sicknes health is growne,	pattern 2
Our shame is veild, this now remaines alone	pattern 2
For us, since he was ours, that wee bee not our owne.	pattern 3

(III, 29)

The stanza also exemplifies paradox, one of the most important and heavily used stylistic features of the poem—and of the whole era for that matter. Paradox appears in many forms in the poem. Above, it not only is the principal concept underlying the stanza but also finds technical support in the caesuras. It appears in the oxymorons, which have been mentioned ("restless rest"), and in the antithetical constructions and statements. Beyond this device is the religious significance—the paradoxes of Christianity—reflected in the following description of Satan:

> All that he speakes (and all he speakes are lies)
> Are oracles, 'tis he (that wounded all)
> Cures all their wounds, he (that put out their eyes)
> That gives them light, he (that death first did call
> Into the world) that with his orizall,
> Inspirits earth: he heav'ns al-seeing eye,
> He earths great Prophet, he, whom rest doth flie,
> That on salt billowes doth, as pillowes, sleeping lie.
> (I, 24)

Christianity, of course, abounds in paradoxes. They are revealed in Scripture, dogmas, beliefs, mysteries of faith: for example, in the fortunate fall, in Christ's death to give man eternal life, in the Trinity (One God, Three Persons), in Foreknowledge and Free Will, and in many more. They are as old as Christianity and as traditional. However, few literary works manifest them so fundamentally as *Christ's Victorie*.

The heavily figurative language in Giles' poem centers in the conceit (that strained or farfetched analogy, discussed previously):

> heav'n it selfe shall slide,
>> And rowle away like melting starres, that glide
>> Along their oylie threads. (I, 38)

Christ's legs are described,

>> As two white marble pillars that uphold
>> Gods holy place whear he in glorie sets,
>>
>> . . .
>>
>> Vein'd every whear with azure rivulets. (II, 13)

Epic or Homeric similes lend special loftiness and the flavor of eloquence, as in this description of Mercy's persuasive power:

>> Like as the thirstie land, in summers heat,
>> Calls to the clouds, and gapes at everie showre,
>> As though her hungry clifts all heav'n would eat,
>> Which if high God into her bosome powre,
>> Though much refesht, yet more she could devoure:
>>> So hang the reedie ears of Angels sweete,
>>> And every breath a thousand cupids meete,
>> Some flying in, some out, and all about her fleet. (I, 49)

Still other rhetorical devices that Giles likes to use include allegorsis
(allegory), personification, hyperbole, apostrophe, classical similes,
various forms of animism (like pathetic fallacy). His use of diction,
however, demands special comment.

In terms of the controversies over the nature of the English
language which raged during the sixteenth century, Fletcher would
have been considered liberal. In diction, he freely coins neologisms,
or "inkhorn" terms, as the purists called them. Literary English of
the Renaissance seems today distinctly Latinate, but Giles appears
less obvious and extreme than many, including Milton. However,
Shelden claims the following original coinages for Giles: "coetan,"
"corylets," "dires" (furies), "furt" (theft), "globe" (solid, compact
mass as of soldiers), "lime" (file), "orbicles," "origialls," and
"sideriall." Although Giles is clearly less prone to employ archaisms
than was Spenser, he does employ archaic inflections—need*en*,
car*en*, *e*longing, *e*blazon—and occasional straining for archaic
effect:

And well I wot, my rime, albee unsmooth,
Ne, saies but what it meanes, ne meanes but sooth,
Ne harmes the good, ne good to harmefull person dooth. (IV, 26)

Another rhetorical device Giles likes is catachresis, or intentional misuse of words; for example, "disadvaunce" (II, 3, 7,), "congies" (II, 4, 2), or "belamours" (IV, 48, 3). The last word illustrates also his unusual anglicizing of foreign words, as in "whear beawties *indeflourishing* abide" (I, 46, 2). He seems to compound freely (perhaps influenced in this direction by Du Bartas): "over-prayed," "over-swell," "over-moos't," "up-plowed," "after-sorrowe," "over-wooed." In short, Giles' diction for special effects or for enrichment is quite liberal; it is far less extreme and mannered, however, than his use of other rhetorical devices.

Analysis of stanza 48 reveals the complexity of the technique and art of combining rhetorical devices to make "the golden phrases flie":

1   As melting hony, dropping from the combe,
2   So still the words, that spring between thy lipps
3   Thy lippes, whear smiling sweetnesse keepes her home,
4   And heavenly Eloquence pure manna sippes,
5   He that his pen but in that fountaine dipps
6   How nibly will the golden phrases flie,
7   And shed forth streames of choycest rhetorie,
8   Welling celestiall torrents out of poesie? (I, 48)

The poet focuses the entire description of Mercy's persuasive power on a single, small feature—her words (l. 2). He elaborately develops this feature through a series of overlapping conceits that build and expand like an inverse pyramid. Her "words" are first "melting honey" (l. 1: a simile, a conceit, and the key sensuous analogy that is therefore placed first); the "lippes" from which the words "spring" become the home of Sweetness (l. 3: a personification and conceit) and the dining room where "Eloquence" sips manna (l. 4: another personification and conceit in which manna-honey extends the analogy to the anagogical level). The words / mouth become also a *fountain* of "golden phrases" (l. 5: another conceit) from which issues *"streames* of choycest rhetorie" (l. 7: another conceit) and wells and torrents of celestial poetry (l. 8: two more conceits). All the conceits have to do with liquid, and each develops as an enlargement: *melting, sips, fountain, streams, wells, torrents.* Additional adornments include anadiplosis (3 - 4), alliteration, and so forth.

The art in this stanza, and throughout the poem, involves extensive development and elaboration of particulars into complex but highly controlled patterns. In describing Mercy's persuasive powers, Fletcher starts with a single detail, "the words," which he develops into an elaborate symbol of the whole; this technique exemplifies his whole manner of celebrating Christ. He starts with only four main events, but these, like the words, are developed elaborately, ornately, extensively, even fantastically. The devices of rhetoric become finally the means to a greater end: language blocks with which to build an elaborate poetic structure.

II *Style and Art: General*

From this stanza, one can also abstract with little difficulty an equation which characterizes, intentionally or not, Giles' poem. Poetry equals celestial torrents of choicest rhetoric, golden phrases *(melting honey)* of eloquence. A final ingredient, *wit*, holds it all together. Basically, *wit* meant ingenuity, especially mental and verbal ingenuity. Wit, a notable feature of *Christ's Victorie and Triumph*, is also stamped all over the poem's prefatory verses that were written by Phineas and Francis Nethersole:

> Nor can I so much say as much I ought,
> Nor yet so little can I say as nought.
>
> Fond ladds, that spend so fast your poasting time,
> (Too poasting time, that spends your time as fast).

Nethersole, in fact, speaks directly of Giles' "flood of wit." Giles himself uses the term regularly in "To the Reader": "as though poetrie corrupted all good witts, when indeed, bad witts corrupt poetrie." That Giles would "sing divine and heroical matters" as a *vates* in a highly rhetorical, witty, and seemingly artificial manner is not entirely strange, however. Both Phineas and Nethersole speak of "the highest pitch." Rhetoric was the supreme art of persuasion, eloquence, and sublimity; and there is a kind of hierarchical logic in celebrating the loftiest subject (God) through the quintessence of eloquence (rhetoric).

Although most modern commentators declare Spenser to be Giles' master or his major source or influence, Spenser exhibits almost none of this kind of "wit" and little of these rhetorical extremes. In one way or another, Spenser influenced almost everyone of the age including Giles Fletcher; for he was, in fact, England's great prosodist whose concerns with musical qualities in poetic language, with poetry as a speaking picture (*ut pictura poesis*), drew many subsequent poets to their calling. "A Canto Upon Eliza" shows his influence upon Giles. *Christ's Victorie and Triumph* seems to have drawn both sustenance and source material, as previously noted, from both the *Fowre Hymnes* and *The Faerie Queene*. However, it imitates neither. The second book, "Christ's Victorie on Earth," comes closest to imitation: it appears indebted to *The Faerie Queene* in mode, manner, episode, allegory, and style. However, the overall verse texture of *Christ's Victorie and Triumph*, as well as its impact upon the reader as a finished piece of art, is quite distinct. Furthermore, Giles' style can be related even more fruitfully to yet other stylistic trends of the age.[2]

The grand or ciceronian style in prose, especially as practiced by John Lyly (1554 - 1606), is one such trend. Lyly's famous euphuistic prose, which was the rage of court society in the 1580s and 1590s, was only the most exaggerated version of the grand style: it was the most rhetorically extreme instance of the Renaissance love of magnificence, of the high and noble, fittingly expressed. Although Lyly's *Euphues: The Anatomy of Wit* (1578) and *Euphues and His England* (1580) were the most popular successes of the age, they were also highly moralistic, educational, even pious and nationalistic. *Euphues* combined "wit," verbal-rhetorical ingenuity, and learning in a fresh and startling way. That style appears to have influenced Giles' work in *Christ's Victorie and Triumph*. The first page of *Euphues* contains a well-known example of that style:

This young gallant, of more wit than wealth, and more wealth than wisdom, seeing himself inferior to none in pleasant conceits, thought himself superior to all in honest conditons, insomuch that he deemed himself so apt to all things that he gave himself almost to nothing but practicing of those things commonly which are incident to these sharp wits, fine phrases, smooth quipping, merry taunting, using jesting without mean, and abusing mirth without measure. As therefore the sweetest rose hath his prickle, the finest velvet his brack, the fairest flour his bran, so the sharpest wit hath his wanton will, and the holiest head his wicked way.

The extensive parallelism (isocolon, parison, paromoion), the alliterations, sententiae, repetition, and rhetorical extremes reflected in this passage by Lyly are earmarks of the style that Giles used in his prose "Dedication" to Dean Nevile:

As I have alwaies thought the place wherein I live, after heaven, principally to be desired, both because I most want, and it most abounds with wisdome, which is fled by some with as much delight, as it is obtained by others, and ought to be followed by all: so I cannot but next unto God, for ever acknowledge myselfe most bound unto the hand of God, (I meane yourselfe) that reacht downe, as it were out of heaven, unto me, a benefit of that nature, and price, then which, I could wish none, (onely heaven itselfe excepted) either more fruitfull, and contenting for the time that is now present, or more comfortable, and encouraging for the time that is alreadie past, or more hopefull, and promising for the time that is yet to come.

The ease with which such prose can be turned into verse like Giles Fletcher's is easily demonstrated by merely printing the following prose example from *Euphues* in verse form:

> Alexander valiant in war, yet given to wine.
> Tully eloquent in his glosses, yet vainglorious.
> Solomon wise, yet too too wanton
> David holy but yet an homicide.
> None more witty than Euphues,
> Yet at the first none more wicked.
> The freshest colors soonest fade,
> The keenest razor soonest turneth his edge,
> The finest cloth is soonest eaten with moths.

One may also compare this passage in verse structure and syntax with the following selection from *Christ's Victorie and Triumph:*

> Whear all are rich, and yet no gold they owe,
> An all are Kings, and yet no Subjects knowe,
> I look for glorie, but finde miserie;
> I look for joy, but finde a sea of teares;
> I looke that we should live and finde him die;
> Christ suffers, and in this, his teares begin;
> Suffers for us, and our joy springs in this,
> Suffers to death, here is his Manhood seen,
> Suffers to rise, and here his Godhead is.[3]

Or one may compare Lyly's passage with still another stanza from
Christ's Victorie and Triumph:

> No Sorrowe nowe hangs clowding on their browe,
> No bloodles Maladie empales their face,
> No Age drops on their hayrs his silver snowe,
> No Nakednesse their bodies doeth embase,
> No Povertie themselves, and theirs disgrace,
> No fear of death the joy of life devours,
> No unchast sleepe their precious time deflowrs,
> No losse, no griefe, no change waite on their
>   winged hour's. (IV, 35)

Since both Phineas Fletcher and Francis Nethersole use the same
style as Giles in their prefatory verse to *Christ's Victorie and
Triumph,* its choice by all three must have been deliberate.

Another possible influence on Giles' style might well have been
Giovanni Baptista Marini (1569 - 1625), the literary lion of Italy,
whose influence may have come through Sanazaro or the other
Italians whom Giles mentions in "To the Reader." Marini self-
consciously turned to religious poetry (the kind that Giles would
later write); he became celebrated for a style that turned upon sensuous details, symbols, and violently extreme rhetoric; and
Marinism, of considerable importance in Europe may have been an
influence upon Spenser, but it clearly affected Crashaw and other
English writers later in the seventeenth century. It has been identified with the new stylistic tendencies in European art and
literature that are most commonly called Baroque.

Despite the difficulties of trying to apply a term taken from the
fine arts of Italy in the sixteenth century to the literature of England
in the seventeenth century, the term Baroque provides a useful way
of distinguishing the feature of Giles' poem from Spenser's. Since
these features also seem synonymous with new trends in English
literature around the turn of the century, the term serves double
duty in designating an emergent period style.

In art, the counter-Reformation movement in sixteenth-century
Italy led among other things to direct treatment of the life of Christ
and the martyrs and saints as well as to renewed attention to
religious subjects generally. In literature, the same treatment can be
seen in the works of Marini, Sanazaro, Andreini, and other Baroque
writers. *Christ's Victorie* is the first such poem to appear in English

and in England. Its style, as with other Baroque religious poems, reflects the effort to make art function to the ends of religion—to focus all the resources of art and rhetoric upon a subject for essentially devotional purposes. Such features in Giles' poem as heavy reliance on rhetoric, on sensuous details, on tension of conflicting forces, the use of paradox, hyperbole, extreme elaboration of metaphor (particularly conceit), wit, and rich ornamentation are characteristics of Baroque literary art.[4] *Christ's Victorie and Triumph* is then the first Baroque Christian heroic poem in England; it ushers in a new age. After it march a host of related works by Phineas Fletcher, Joseph Fletcher (unrelated), Cowley, Milton, Bunyan, Crashaw, and many more. Christian heroic poetry was one of the notable literary accomplishments of seventeenth-century England.

In fact, Giles Fletcher appears to have been in the forefront of a number of new literary waves that were just beginning to sweep across the English literary scene; for the stylistic features of *Christ's Victorie and Triumph* appear afterwards in other prominent writers of the seventeenth century. Wit, conceits, paradox, and hyperbole are earmarks also of Donne's style and work (to some extent of all the Metaphysicals). One may compare, for example, the following description of Christ on the cross by Fletcher with that by Donne:

> See whear the author of all life is dying:
> O fearefull day! he dead, what hope of living?
> See whear the hopes of all our lives are buying:
> O chearfull day! they bought, what feare if grieving?
> Love love for hate, and death for life is giving:
>   Loe how his armes are stretch't abroad to grace thee,
>   And, as they open stand, call to embrace thee,
> Why stai'st thou then soule; o flie, flie thither
>   hast thee. (*CVT*, III, 34)

In "Good Friday, 1613" (three years after *Christ's Victorie*), Donne wrote:

> There I should see a Sunne, by rising set,
> And by that setting endlesse day beget;
> But that Christ on this Crosse, did rise and fall,
> Sin had eternally benighted all

. . .

> Could I behold those hands which span the Poles,
> And tune all spheares at once, peirc'd with those holes?

The same kind of graphic, detailed images, so characteristic of Baroque art, appear in like passages from Giles and George Herbert when they describe the crucifixion:

> His radious head, with shamefull thornes they teare,
> His tender backe, with bloody whipps they rent,
> His side and heart, they furrowe with a spear,
> His hands, and feete, with riving nayles they tent.
> (CVT, III, 35)
> A Man so wrung with pains, that all His hair,
> His skinne, His garments bloudie be. . . .
> And taste that juice which, on the crosse, a pike
> Did set again abroach; then let him say.
> ("The Agonie")

However, Richard Crashaw's work (strongly influenced also by Marini) contains the most striking likeness to Giles' style and poem. In terms of conceits which are conspicuously embodied in sensuous details, the resemblance is particularly strong. Here is Crashaw, for example, "On the Bleeding Wounds of our Crucified Lord" which one may compare to the preceding description by Giles:

> Jesu, no more! it is full tide
>   From thy hands and from they feet,
> From thy head, and from thy side,
>   All thy *Purple Rivers* meet.
> But o thy side! thy deepe dig'd side
>   That hath a double Nilus going.
> Not a haire but payes his River
>   To this Red Sea of thy blood.

Or one may compare the following description of Christ by Giles to that of Mary Magdalene by Crashaw:

> His cheekes as snowie apples, sop't in wine,
> Had their red roses quencht with lillies white,
> And like to garden strawberries did shine,
> Wash't in a bowle of milke, or rose-buds bright
> Unbosoming their brests against the light.
> (II, 11)

> O cheeks! Bedds of chast loves
> By your own showres seasonably dash't,
>   Eyes! nests of milky doves
>   In your own wells decently washt,
> O wit of love! that thus could place
> Fountain and Garden in one face.
>
>   ("The Weeper")[5]

In Fletcher and Crashaw, the extremes of rhetorical wit, hyperbole, metaphoric exaggeration, sensuousness, and florid coloration find like voices. Moreover, both poets worked these extremities of style toward the same end: devotional or liturgical experience and religious exaltation.

What Milton saw in *Christ's Victorie,* however, appears to have been less the style than the new subject matter and the treatment of it. For example, Milton's "On the Morning of Christ's Nativity" bears numerous resemblances to *Christ's Victorie and Triumph* in incidents, details, figures, and verse stanza as well as in scattered phrases. It, too, is full of paradox and celebrates the Nativity in terms of the larger story of Christian divine history. Milton's fragment, "The Passion," seems to owe something to Book III, of "Christ's Victorie over Death." *Paradise Regained*, which deals with the Temptation of Christ in the wilderness, was surely modeled upon "Christ's Victorie on Earth." *Paradise Lost* seems indebted in many ways, large and small, to the whole of Giles' *Christ's Victorie and Triumph.*

Undoubtedly, Milton was also influenced by larger, more nebulous matters in *Christ's Victorie and Triumph.* As has been observed, the concept of *vates* underlies both of their pronouncements about poetry. Much of the seriousness, the dedication, the intensity of Giles' poem reappears in Milton's work. Finally, aside from other features of style and content, *Christ's Victorie and Triumph* and most of Milton's religious poems share one other large quality of Baroque art—its eclecticism.[6]

III *Criticism*

Critical response to *Christ's Victory and Triumph* over the centuries has been on the whole very uneven and quite diverse in type and quality. Extant seventeenth-century responses tend to be biographical and general, like those by Thomas Fuller and William

Winstanley, rather than critical and analytical. The period of the late seventeenth and early eighteenth centuries witnessed the rise of criticism as well as a distinct change of literary tastes; and neoclassical critics found little of value in Baroque or religious poets. Giles Fletcher and his *Christ's Victorie and Triumph* disappeared from the literary scene until the very end of the century when the critics developed a general renaissance of interest in "ancient" poetry. However, during the nineteenth century Giles' work received considerable attention and a variety of critical responses.

Robert Willmott in *Lives of the Sacred Poets* (London, 1834) takes the position, for example, that *Christ's Victorie and Triumph* has large flaws but beauty in parts: "It has not the lustre of one great luminous whole, unbroken in the purity of its splendour; its brilliancy is dazzling, but fragmentary [p. 56]. . . . Fletcher's want of art [is] in the composition of his poem and of order in the narrative. The third book is particularly open to this objection; some parts, however, are very sublime. The traitor Judas . . . is worthy the pencil of Michael Angelo." However, when comparing *Christ's Victorie and Triumph* with Milton's *Paradise Regained*, Willmot provides a context for his previous remarks and grows more affirmative: "In Scriptural simplicity of conception, and in calm and sustained dignity of tone, the palm of superiority must be awarded to Milton; while in fertility of fancy, earnestness of devotion, and melody of expression, Fletcher may be said to stand, at least, upon an equality with him" (p. 56).

S. C. Hall, who echoes Wilmott in part, adds, however, some negative criticism in his *The Book of Gems: The Poets and Artists of Great Britain* (London, 1848):

Of *Christ's Victory* we may speak in terms of the highest praise. The Poet has exhibited a fertility of invention and a rich store of fancy, worthy of the sublime subject. The style is lofty and energetic, the descriptions natural and graphic, and the construction of the verse graceful and harmonious. But unhappily he has introduced among his sacred themes—the birth, temptation, passion, resurrection and ascension of the Saviour—so many characters from and allusions to profane history, as often to jar upon the sense and to render the poet justly liable to the charges of bad taste and inconsistency. Giles Fletcher indeed had no power in selecting his thoughts, or his reputation might have equalled his genius.

The charge of "bad taste" recurs from time to time during the century. George MacDonald, for example, in *England's Antiphon*

(London, *c.* 1868) notes, "No doubt there are here touches of exrable taste, such as the punning trick with *man* and *manners,* suggesting a false antithesis. . . . The passage is fine and powerful, notwithstanding its faults and obscurities." On the whole, however, most cf the criticism of the period is distinctly affirmative. Ezekiel Sanford, editor, comments upon "a tone of enthusiasn peculiarly solemn"; the poet Robert Southey says that "the single poem which he [Giles] has left, will preserve his name while there is any praise"; an anonymous reviewer of an 1835 edition of Giles' poem states that "his poetry never lacks ornament. The page is sprinkled all over like a field of violets. The verse moves along stately and liquid, freighted with close thought and earnest moral sense"; the Reverend R. Cattermole, editor of the twenty-one volume *Sacred Classics,* calls *Christ's Victorie and Triumph* "a work of extraordinary merit and interest," and then quotes another critic: "sublimity of sentiment, opulence of description, and harmony of numbers."[7]

The most visible critic of Giles' poem and of the poet during the nineteenth century, however, was clearly Alexander B. Grosart, the editor of Giles' complete poems in 1869. Grosart is unmistakably zealous about establishing Giles' true place among the "worthies"; however, beside some florid exaggeration, he left in his "Memorial Introduction" some criticism that is well worth attending:

> Altogether I pronounce GILES FLETCHER to be a true "Maker" in the full, creative sense, and a "Singer" inevitable as a bird, and "Christ's Victorie" in its fourfold wholeness, a complete Poem and as a work of art, a "perfect chrysolite." Some of the facets—to pursue the second figure—may perchance be unskillfully cut, and the light broken in consequence: but the consummate jewel is there "shooting its sparks at Phoebus." It is original and definite in its conception. Its conception is noble. Its execution fulfills (-fills full) its conception. Throughout, it is marked by compression: compressed, purged thought, compressed learning, compressed imagination. Everywhere you have the sense of power in reserve, resources undrawn on. With few exceptions, he is sustained in his loftiest flights. . . . "Christ's Victorie" can never die save with the language: but our generation would profit by familiarity with it. It will live on and be unhurt; neglecters of it lose. (pp. 91 - 2)

All of Grosart's characteristic enthusiasm, unrestrained appreciation, and personal tastes are voiced in the following passage:

The intensity of the Poet's own Love and Faith, Hope and Graciousness lies over his Poem—like a bar of sunlight—as one has seen such shattering itself in dazzling glory against a heath-purpled mountain-side. In unexpected turns, in equally unexpected places, you are reminded that you have no mere Singer working artistically but a "Saint"—in the Biblical not Medieval meaning—pouring out the glad Worship of his whole nature—a nature rich of faculty in itself and enriched with celestial riches. (pp. 55 - 6)

Twentieth-century critics of the poem (like twentieth-century criticism generally) have varied even more extremely in response than the nineteenth-century critics. For one thing, more negative views have been expressed. W. J. Courthope in *A History of English Poetry* (London, 1903), finds, for example, "Giles' impersonations suffer from a different fault. He mixes his abstractions with real personages." Courthope dislikes Giles' "astonishing want of judgment in Christ with 'snowie cheekes' " ("the luxuriousness of Marini") as well as his "passion for coining new words [as strong] as any member of the French Pleiad" (pp. 141 - 4). H. E. Cory in his lengthy discussion is usually negative but he occasionally rises to the kind of mixed reaction that is reflected in Douglas Bush's comment: "uneven but often beautiful work."[8]

Joan Grundy, in *The Spenserian Poets* (London, 1969), the most recent critic to deal at length with Giles Fletcher, Jr., is strongly favorable; she also minimizes the "Spenserianism" in his work: "*Christs Victorie and Triumph* is, formally a very fluid work, almost druidical in its capacity to flow from one literary form to another. Thus although there are Spenserian echoes throughout, the second book is the only one extensively to adopt Spenser's Method." She strongly underlines, as did Grosart, the intensity and sense of rapture in the poem. For example, she writes about the apocalyptic conclusion of the work that "The description of the triumph of Christ and the joys of the New Jerusalem with which the poem ends is one of the most sustained passages of poetic rapture to be found anywhere, and it is, most of it, magnificent" (p. 199).

Most of the scholar-critics of the twentieth century have tended to judge the work in relation to its place in the literary history of the period. Frank Warnke, for example, finds *Christ's Victorie* one of "the three most significant epic or quasi-epic poems between *The Faerie Queene* and *Paradise Lost*. Of these, Fletcher's work strikes the modern reader as the most accessible" (p. 709). When Warnke, Grundy, and many others relate their discussions and evaluations of the poem to Baroque art and literature, they are in accord with what is probably the dominant critical trend of the last twenty years. Grundy writes, "Actually the most strikingly Baroque part of Fletcher is his visual imagination. Many of the pictorial and descriptive effects he achieves vividly recall the work of Baroque artists, of Bernini, Rubens, Gentileschi, and others. . . . It is a precise visual detail . . . from similar details in Baroque paintings and frescos" (p. 199). M. M. Mahood in *Poetry and Humanism* (Oxford, 1950) also exemplifies this emphasis: "Like every Baroque work of devotional art, Fletcher's poem directs the impulses of humanism to the end of faith" (p. 171). Mahood also relates a number of the specific features of the poem to Baroque art, such as the rich ornamentation, turbulence, tension of conflicting forces (sense and spirit, time and eternity, attainment and desire), paradox; and he finds a certain intellectual tempering, a sharp metaphysical wittiness not found in the work's Elizabethan models" (p. 172). All these aspects of Baroque art he relates to qualities in Jesuit emblemata as well as to the lyrics of Donne, Herbert, and Crashaw.[9]

IV *Commentary*

Over the centuries, *Christ's Victorie and Triumph* has elicited numerous and varied critical responses. Even a cursory investigation of them reveals at least one large generalization: most of the notably negative critics revealed a correspondingly strong dislike for eclectic art; the strongest adherents revealed the opposite. Most critics have agreed about the prominent features of the poem, but they have valued them differently: for example, D. C. Shelden writes:

Fletcher's rhetoric and general poetic style are scarcely less exasperating than his diction. He is constantly betrayed into extravagancies by his striving after wit, and not seldom loses sight of what he is doing in order to achieve some subordinate figure. The rhetorical devices which in a greater poet would be used to contribute to some particular effect are, in Fletcher, constantly pursued as an end in themselves, without regard for larger poetic significance.

R. Anderson writes:

His *Christ's Victorie and Triumph*, a poem rich and picturesque in the highest degree, deserves to be better known. It is on a much happier subject than that of his brother's, and merits the attention of the reader of poetry, for energy of style, sublimity of sentiment, opulence of description, and harmony of number. Such fertility of fancy, such exuberance of imagery, such felicity of expression, rival everything of the kind in the poetry of his age.[10]

The style, structure, and technique of *Christ's Victorie and Triumph* are unmistakably distinct. The poem, unique in very obvious ways, draws forth strong and extreme responses from many readers. One can relate the sensibilities behind the two opposite views that are reflected by Shelden and Anderson to dominant types of art in the seventeenth century itself. The extreme detractors seem to value the simplicity, regularity, and harmony of "high renaissance" art and to excoriate Baroque art as eccentric, artificially novel, contorted. The extreme adherents, like Grosart, simply reverse it.

One additional possibility not yet suggested about the poem must be mentioned. It appears quite likely that the four parts of the poem were composed in a different order and at different periods. The original design and Book II are most likely work of 1603 - 05 when Giles was most heavily influenced by Spenser (the period of "A Canto Upon Eliza"). The composition of Book I, which is less Spenserian, followed that of Book II. Several years later, about 1608 - 09, after reading the recently published translation of Du Bartas by Sylvester and in anticipation of his own Ordination, Giles wrote Books III and IV. They are like Du Bartas, especially in their sermonlike construction and are un-Spenserian. In general, the first two books reflect late Medieval, early Renaissance conceptions, conventions, and structures. The last two books reflect more the features of Baroque art; and "Henri," written two years later, develops these Baroque characteristics even further. In the revision of the whole poem for publication about 1610, the Baroque flavor of Giles' later style also found its way into the verse texture of books I and II; but inconsistencies remain.

This speculation may help to explain the peculiar type of unevenness and the extreme degree of eclecticism in the poem as well as the curious pattern of critical response to it. However, the rise and fall of its critical reception over the centuries is also clearly relatable to changing tastes. Indeed, through most of the first half of the present century, *Christ's Victorie and Triumph* was neglected or treated unsympathetically. The work of Spenser and Milton, to which it bears obvious affinities, has undergone similar although less extreme treatment. However, the last twenty years has witnessed a renewed interest in eclectic and Baroque art as well as a revived appreciation. The atmosphere now exists for more sympathetic reading and for fresh appraisal.

Where weak, the poem seems either too conceptualized or else overly embellished: where excessive artifice and rhetorical filler replace substance; where sensuous strings of word-sounds replace sense; and where ornamentation obfuscates the subject. The poem seems strongest and best when it is viewed as an heroic celebration of Christ in an essentially nonnarrative, nonrepresentational mode. The poem's tremendous dedication and seriousness of purpose are striking; and, when rhetoric and emotion correspond, the poetry becomes impressive indeed, flowering in flamboyance, flourish, courage, occasional brilliance, and individuality, which is everywhere apparent—especially the eclectic kind.

Furthermore, credit also must be given to Giles Fletcher, Jr. for the position of *Christ's Victorie and Triumph* as the forerunner, if not the innovator, of a whole new literary style at the beginning of the seventeenth century in England. The poem is an excellent, although not totally successful, example of a new type of literature, often labeled Baroque.

In an age noted for its many excellent minor poets, Giles Fletcher, Jr. reveals impressive poetic skills. It is difficult, finally, not to agree with Grosart when he writes of the poem, "our generation would profit by familiarity with it. It will live on and be unhurt; neglectors of it lose."

CHAPTER 5

Phineas Fletcher: Young Poet of Cambridge

I "The Kentish lad . . . His oaen reed"[1]

SUPERFICIALLY, the life of Phineas Fletcher seems much like that of his younger brother Giles, although he lived almost twice as long. The elder son was born and baptized at the family center in Cranbrook, Kent, in April, 1582. Like Giles, Jr., Phineas spent his boyhood in Cranbrook and London, but the rural rather than urban home remained central to his poetic consciousness. He followed his father's footsteps to Eton and then onward to King's College, Cambridge. In 1600, Phineas was elected Scholar and commenced an academic career which lasted fifteen years. Its high points included Bachelor of Arts (1604); Master of Arts (1607 - 08); Ordination, Bachelor of Divinity, and Fellowship (1611).

However, in late 1612 his future career at King's College became doubtful. He took an extended leave from the college for over a year and a half. He returned to residency in 1614, produced there his play *Sicelides* in 1615, but left shortly afterwards, ending his university career. For the next five years, he appears to have lived perhaps as chaplain, with the family of Sir Henry Willoughby at Risley Hall, Derbyshire. He married Elizabeth Vincent in August, 1615, at Wilne, Derbyshire, a few miles from Risley Hall. In 1621, he became rector of the church at Hilgay, Norfolk (the living from which was owned by Willoughby), a position that he retained for the remainder of his life (until 1650).

Phineas, who wrote throughout his life, left behind a body of literature larger than that of most of his Renaissance contemporaries; in fact, his work rivals in size the canons of Spenser and Milton, the two literary giants of the period. The collected works of Phineas Fletcher include three volumes of religious prose, an epic,

77

an epyllion, a drama, several medium-length verse narratives, pastoral eclogues, verse epistles, epithalamia, hymns, psalms, translations, various songs, occasional pieces, lyrics, and devotional poems. In scope, variety, and quantity, his canon is second to none of that age.

Phineas draws attention to himself as a poet in a highly self-conscious way. He saw himself, however, as a very different kind of poet from his brother Giles, for, like Spenser, whom he admired, he chose to model himself on Vergil. Vergil, who had long been recognized as one of the greatest Roman poets, had begun and had become famous by writing pastoral poems, the *Bucolics* or *Eclogues*. In his *Georgics*, he continued to laud the happy rural life but did so in longer poems. His last work, the great epic, *The Aeneid*, was not only his most famous poem, but also his longest. Spenser too began with pastoral eclogues in *The Shepheardes Calender* and ended with the epic, *The Faerie Queene*. Fletcher quite clearly and consciously followed that pattern. As he wrote in an early pastoral poem," To my beloved Thenot" (a pastoral character in Spenser's *The Shepheardes Calender*),

> Two shepherds I adore with humble love;
> Th' high-towring swain, that by slow Mincius waves
> His well-grown wings at first did lowly prove,
> Where *Corydon's* sick love full sweetly raves;
> But after sung bold *Turnus* daring braves:
> And next our nearer *Colins* sweetest strain;
> Most, where he most his *Rosalind* doth plain.
> Well, may I after look, but follow all in vain.
>   (St. 3)

His reference to Corydon of Vergil's *Bucolics* and to Colin of Spenser's *The Shepheardes Calender* underscores the fact that, like Vergil and Spenser, Phineas would start writing poetry of the pastoral world and mode. His first published poem, in fact, was a pastoral, its singing shepherd was "Coridon."

Pastoralism, whatever modern readers may think of it, was more than an artificial literary convention to the era and to Phineas Fletcher. The literary tradition, especially as embodied in the form of the eclogue, was outlined neatly and chronologically by "E. K." in the "Epistle Prefatory" of *The Shepheardes Calender* (1579): "So flew Theocritus, as you may perceive he was all ready full fledged. So flew Virgile, as not yet well feeling his winges. So flew Mantuane, as being not full somd. So Petrarque. So Boccace; So Marot,

Sanazarus, and also divers other excellent both Italian and French Poetes, whose foting this Author [Spenser] every where followeth."[2] So "flew". Phineas Fletcher, and had he needed additional guidance, the elaborate glosses by "E. K." to each of the twelve eclogues of *The Shepheardes Calender* provided detailed reference to every large and small aspect of the pastoral tradition.

The pastoral world offered more than an idealized natural world of universal truth to the Renaissance poet. Under the guise of the lowly shepherd, he could safely express his personal feelings, his particular religious and political beliefs, his hopes and fears about his art; and, he could discuss his relationships to friends, family, and enemies. In short, the pastoral poet could be personal and subjective while appearing to be universal and objective. The Colins, Thenots, Thomalins, Rosalinds, Elizas, and Thirsils were idealized rustics as well as close friends, lovers, relatives, monarchs. And nobody could be certain where the "feigning" of the poet left off and where reality began—except perhaps the intimates of the poet. In an artificial world of poetry, music, and other arts, the past and present, the ideal and the real, all came together. Since the poet and his friends were protected by their pastoral masks and disguises from the recriminations of powerful men, they enjoyed a kind of public freedom of speech while they played a very private, intimate, poetic game. Furthermore, the obvious correspondence in a "Shepherd" world of both classical and Christian symbols and meanings made the whole mode particularly appealing to Christian-Humanists of the Renaissance.

However, the social rather than religious aspects of pastoralism occupied the young poet Phineas Fletcher at Cambridge. His own life, his friends, and his own sense of being a poet comprised the subjects of his pastoral verses. Cambridge, "our Chame, and Cambridge Muses," clearly dominated both his life and his poetry from about 1600 - 1615. The Cam River symbolizes the place and the life, the "oaten reed" symbolizes the pastoral poet, just as had the river Mincius and the "reed" for Vergil. Even in Phineas' first published poem, in *Sorrowes Joy* (1603), Coridon, whose song "of passed woe, and . . . of present joy" forms the body of the poem, must announce to King James I:

> And sing I will, though I sing sorrily,
> And thee, though little, I will glorifie,
> And shrilly pipe aloud, the whilst my Chame
> Shall answer all againe, thy name aye lives.

Phineas' Cambridge world involved a number of relatives, friends, and acquaintances who can be identified, as well as related to the pastoral figures who people his poems during this period. Phineas gives the very strong impression that there was a literary group of which he was the center. The group included, of course, Giles, Jr.; and Phineas wrote of their relationship, "souls self-same in nearer love did grow: / So seem'd two joyn'd in one, or one disjoyn'd in two." His father, with whose career at Cambridge and with whose role as a poet Phineas strongly identified, is the "Thelgon" of the poems. Phineas' best and closest friend, John Tomkins, the organist of King's College and later of St. Paul's, London, a poet of sorts, became the "Thomalin of the pastorals.

Tomkins' even more famous brother, the composer-musician Thomas Tomkins, was also a friend. William Cappell, either a fellow student or Phineas' student, is "Willy." Edmund Cook (E.C.) and William Woodford were both friends of Phineas from Eton and King's. The latter, who was also a poet and a priest, is probably "Dorius." Another Cambridge man Francis Quarles, the author of *Emblems* (1635), one of the most popular works of the century, was a protégé of Princess Elizabeth and a great admirer of Phineas' work; he may be "Thenot." Phineas himself was first "Coridon," then "Myrtil," then "Thirsil," and briefly "Algon." Since he wrote, however, under only one of these pseudonyms at a time, they help to date his poems.[3]

The name "Coridon" comes from Vergil. "Myrtil" a pastoral character in one of Phineas' father's poems, had for Phineas a special association with love and water: "Venus loves myrtils, myrtils love the shore" (*P.E.*, VII, 21). The name "Thirsil" was given to Phineas by "Fusca," his first lady-love, sometime about 1606 - 08, and was his major pastoral pseudonym for many years. As he wrote in "To my beloved Thenot" (ca. 1606 - 8).

>   what e're befall me,
> Or *Myrtil*, (so'fore *Fusca* fair did thrall me,
> Most was I know'n) or now poore *Thirsil* name me,
> *Thirsil*, for so my *Fusca* pleases frame me.

Fusca was from the other world that plays such a large part in Phineas' poetry and life: the world of Kent (of Cranbrook, of Brenchly's Hill, the Medway River, Ide Hill, and Hollingbourn). Not only was this the region of his birth and family, but also that of his relatives like the Sheafes (his mother's family), the Pownalls (his aunt and cousins), the Robarts (his cousins), and friends like Lady Culpepper of Hollingbourn, her daughter Elizabeth, and Elizabeth Irby. Phineas not only visited Kent during vacations but wrote regularly to his friends there. They became part of his pastoral coterie along with his Cantabrigians; and Kent became an extension of Cambridge.

II   *Poems, 1603 - 10*

The poems which were written during the sunshine years of Phineas' career, 1603 - 10, reflect the picture of a young poet who is intoxicated by the idea of poetry; who is very preoccupied with his role as poet, with his friends, his life; and who is busy making pastoral poetry from it all. "To my Beloved Thenot in answer to his verse" is a verse-epistle in the pastoral mode; in four eight-line stanzas it describes his admiration for Vergil and Spenser and their pastorals, his pastoral names, and his love of Fusca ("My *Fusca's* eyes, my *Fusca's* beauty dittying").

Fusca, the young lady from Kent (possibly Elizabeth Culpepper) who clearly had Phineas' heated devotion for several years (*ca.* 1606 - 10) is mentioned or discussed in six poems to almost as many friends.[4] In "To *E.C.* [Edmund Cook] in *Cambridge,* my sonne by the University," Phineas describes his bittersweet love, "*Fusca's* deep disdain, and Thirsil's plaining":

> Then do not marvel *Kentish* strong delights
> Stealing the time, do here so long detain me:
> Not powerfull *Circe* with her *Hecate* rites,
> Nor pleasing *Lotos* thus could entertain me,
> As *Kentish* powerfull pleasures here enchain me.

In his poem, "To Master W. C." (William Cappell), he tries playfully to lure his "Willy" away from "dainty Nymphs in those retired glades . . . by Haddam" and back to Cambridge; he suggests first,

> By Yellow Chame, where no hot ray shall burn thee,
> Will sit, and sing among the Muses nine;
>
> . . .
>
> We'l read that Mantuan shepherds sweet complaining.

Then worried perhaps that the reading of Vergil by the Cam might
not provide sufficient counter-attraction to the lure of the ladies, he
turns to an example of loving the ladies: "Heare *Thirsil's* moan, and
Fusca's crueltie."

Walter Robarts, Phineas' cousin in Kent, was the recipient of
several verse-epistles in the pastoral mode which speak of Fusca,
but they are more concerned with contrasting the joys of Kent to
the drudgery of Cambridge:

> Here must I stay, in sullen study spent,
> Among our *Cambridge* fennes my time misspending;
> But then revisit our long-long'd-for *Kent*.
> And would my luckie fortune so much grace me,
> As in low *Cranebrook*, or high *Brenchly's* hill,
> Or in some cabin neare thy dwelling place me,
> There would I gladly sport, and sing my fill,
> And teach my tender Muse to raise her quill;

> . . .

> But here among th'unhonour'd willows shade,
> The muddy *Chame* doth me enforced hold.

The first of the verse-epistles, "To my beloved Cousin W. R. Es-
quire," is subtitled "Calend. Januar." (the same as Spenser's first
ecologue of *The Shepheardes Calender*). This pastoral poem relates
the Kent-Cambridge poles to seasonal changes. The six five-line
stanzas develop also in terms of an interesting set of contrasting bird
allusions: parrot, owl, philomel, blackbirds, and day birds versus
night birds. The second, "To my ever honoured Cousin W. R. Es-
quire," develops the same contrast between Kent and Cambridge in
terms of Odysseus' voyage home. The stanzaic pattern, an eight-
line stanza (rhyme royal plus an alexandrine) is that of Giles'
Christ's Victorie.

Walter Robarts' marriage in 1609 to Margaret (Gemma), another
cousin of Fletcher, gave rise to Phineas' exuberant epithalamium:
"An *Hymen* at the Marriage of my most *deare Cousins* Mr. W. and
M. R." The first stanza nicely mirrors the main features of his
poetic, pastoral world during these years:

> *Chamus*, that with thy yellow-sanded stream
> Slid'st softly down where thousand Muses dwell,
> Gracing their bowres, but thou more grac'd by them;

> Heark *Chamus*, from thy low-built greeny cell;
> While all the Nymphs, and all the shepherds sing,
> *Hymen*, oh *Hymen*, here thy saffron garment bring.

The stanzaic pattern is the same one that Phineas used in his verse-epistle to Robarts: *ababccc*, the alexandrine being a refrain. Another brief and typical example from "*An Hymen*," perhaps his poorest poem, illustrates the stylistic weaknesses to which his verse is prone in his pastoral period:

> His breast a shelf of purest alabaster,
> Where *Love's* self sailing often shipwrackt sitteth:
> Hers a twin-rock, unknown but to th' ship-master;
> Which though him safe receives, all other splitteth:
> Both *Love's* high-way, but by *Love's* self unbeaten,
> Most like the milky path which crosses heaven.
> *Hymen*, come *Hymen*; all their marriage joyes are even.

The conceits are notably forced, mixed, and exaggerated in a most unskillful way: the lovers become the Scylla and Charybdis of Love for others; but, together, they form Love's Milky Way. The sound effects in "Love's self sailing often shipwrackt sitteth" are distinctly clumsy. On the whole, the poem is a prosaic and apprentice piece.

III   Piscatorie Eclogues

Phineas' principal and best work during his pastoral period is the *Piscatorie Eclogues,* which was undoubtedly meant to be his major work, and to be equivalent to the *Bucolics* or *Shepheardes Calender.* The *Piscatorie Eclogues* was composed mostly between 1606 - 14, but like most of his work, published much later in 1633. The piscatory forms a small but distinct part of the pastoral tradition. Although Theocritus had included some fisherboys among his shepherds, Sanazaro's piscatory eclogues, mentioned by E. K. among the tradition's "worthies," undoubtedly influenced Phineas more. Phineas, who lists Sanazaro with the "sages," describes him as follows:

> And now of late th' *Italian* fisher-swain
> Sits on the shore to watch his trembling line;
> There teaches rocks and prouder seas to plain
> By *Nesis* fair, and fairer *Mergiline:*
> While this thinne net, upon his oars twin'd.[5]

The reason that Phineas resorted to this singularly slim species of poetry is suggested by a remark in his *The Purple Island:* "What now remains unthought on by those Sages, / Where a new Muse may trie her pineon?" (*P.I.* I, 9). In *English* literature, nobody had either written eclogues or used piscatory paraphernalia for an epic, as Phineas was doing in *The Purple Island.*

In fact, pastoral and piscatory poems are the same except for minor devices and details. In place of the pastoral poem's shepherds, shepherdesses, sheep, staffs, streams, rills, brooks, oaten reeds or pipes, Pan and Arcadian deities, Nymphs, Fawns, and Graces, the reader of the piscatory poem finds fishermen and fisherwomen, nets, poles, boats, oars, seas, shores, baits, waves, sails, Neptune, other related deities, and sea and river nymphs. This piscatory type of pastorialism also has an equally attractive set of Christian religious associations, symbols, and meanings.

Fletcher's *Piscatorie Eclogues,* like the *Bucolics* and *The Shepheardes Calender,* has an important biographical dimension. The seven eclogues have been structured in loosely chronological order by biographical events rather than by the date of their composition, forming a calendar of sorts: I, His father's career; II, Injustices done to Phineas by Cambridge University; III, Love (Coelia); IV, Ministry; V, Love and marriage (Elizabeth Vincent); VI, Love / friendship (Tomkins); VII, Career crossroad: from university poet to priest.

The first eclogue, "Amyntas," features a song by Thelgon (Giles Fletcher, Sr). "Thelgons plaining song," which comprises seventeen of the twenty-two stanzas, presents in piscatory terms a brief life of Giles, Sr. The complaint about loss of friendship and patronage not only has the inherent interest of biography but also shows how closely Phineas empathized with his father's career. As for the eclogue's literary merit, the verse texture and the diction work effectively to promote the story movement and the stanzaic pattern, a variation of rime royal, *ababacc,* is competently handled. A far more accomplished work than "An *Hymen,*" this ecologue was probably written earlier, perhaps in 1606 - 10, clearly before his father's death in 1611 and before Phineas' own trouble at Cambridge in 1612.[6]

Eclogue II, "Thirsil," deals with one of the most traumatic events presented in Phineas' poetry—his forced departure from Cambridge. His bitterest poem, it was written shortly after his father's death and reveals a full awareness that he will have to leave Cambridge. One version, probably the first, is a dialogue between Thirsil (Phineas) and Thomalin (Tomkins). In the published version Phineas adds a framing dialogue between Dorus and Myrtilus in five-line stanzas and excludes one of his most vitriolic slashes at Cambridge, softening somewhat the harshness of the original version. The framing dialogue announces the subject: "Tell we how Thirsil late our seas forswore, / When forc't he left our *Chame*, and desert shore." In the dialogue between Thirsil and Thomalin (twenty stanzas of *ababbccC*; rime royal plus alexandrine), Thirsil makes very clear that the departure is not of his choice: "Not I my *Chame*, but my proud *Chame* refuses." The specifics are then set forth:

> My fish (the guerdon of my toil and pain)
> He [Chamus] causelesse seaz'd, and with ungratefull spite
> Bestow'd upon a lesse deserving swain:
> The cost and labour mine, his all the gain.
> My boat lies broke; my oares crackt, and gone
> Nought has he left me, but my pipe alone.
> (St. 7).

After Thomalin responds with "Ungratefull *Chame!* how oft hath *Thirsil* crown'd / With songs and garlands thy obscurer head?," he asks Cambridge "[who] shall chant thy praise, since Thelgon's lately dead?" The dialogue then develops the details of both the father's and the son's unrewarded efforts and careers at Cambridge, and the poet links their experiences closely and repeatedly through clearly identifiable biographical allusions.

Thirsil delineates no future plans, although there is a vague allusion to "the rock" and "God of seas." The main thrust of the eclogue is denunciatory:

> Thomalin where now doe those nine Muses lye?
> Those Chaster maydes our dangerous shoares doe leave
> Instead of those ambition, flatterie,
> Hate, ryot, wrong, oppression, briberie,
>   Pride high as heav'n, Covetise deepe as hell
>   Are those nine Muses which by Camus dwell.[7]

The biographical aspects of this eclogue clearly outweigh others in interest: the shocked hurt, the bitter awakening, the sudden blackening of his hopes and aspirations are nowhere revealed with such force. The poet's whole idyllic, pastoral-literary world collapsed; and with it his dream. Along with his almost childish recrimination, one finds the pathos of innocence: "Lo your reward . . . / *Chamus* good fishers hate, the Muses selves abuse you."

Eclogue III, "Myrtilus," may well have been the first one written for the *Piscatorie Eclogues;* for Phineas abandoned the pseudonym Myrtil about 1606 - 08. A love complaint to a "Coelia," this poem is written along traditional lines of Courtly Love sentiments, images, and verbal formulas. However, it is so well done that it is overall one of the smoothest of the eclogues. The distance and the detachment of the poet from the experience being recounted effectively promote the lovely artifice of the pastoral idyll.

Eclogue IV, "Chromis," is a dialogue between Thelgon and Chromis about "the fishers trade" (the ministry), and about how it has become "the common badge of scorn and shame"; this poem is the only religious eclogue. For a number of reasons, it appears to have been the last written. The mature, philosophic tone; the six-line stanza *(ababcc)* which Phineas used regularly after leaving Cambridge; the tightness of the style; and the brief appearance of Algon (Phineas' pseudonym after 1615) in the last three stanzas suggest 1620 - 30 as probably the period of composition. Thelgon is Giles, Sr.; Algon, Phineas; and Chromis, a younger poet and priest, who "dost like so well . . . The Prince of fishers," is undoubtedly Giles, Jr.

Chromis mostly laments that the ministry "once highly priz'd" is now so different:

> This is the briefest summe of fishers life,
> To sweat, to freeze, to watch, to fast, to toil,
> Hated to love, to live despis'd, forlorn,
> A sorrow to himself, all others scorn.
> (St. 10)

Thelgon, the older, wiser man who knows the world and especially the court, indicates how many of the clergy have become "a crew of idle grooms" and how the corrupt values of the world flourish. Algon, who traces "our trade" from the disciple-fishermen who were caught originally by *The* "Fisher" and "were fishes made," suggests Christian consolations and ends the poem with a prayer which nicely illustrates the polished style and sure touch of this eclogue:

> Oh Prince of waters, Soveraigne of seas,
> Whom storms & calms, whom windes and waves obey;

> If ever that great Fisher did thee please,
> Chide thou the windes, and furious waves allay:
>> So on thy shore the fisher-boys shall sing
>> Sweet songs of peace to our sweet peaces King.
>
>> (St. 31).

In Eclogue V, "Nicaea," Phineas returns to secular love and more directly to his life:

> The well known fisher-boy, that late his name,
> And place, and (ah for pity!) mirth had changed;
>> Which from the Muses spring, & churlish *Chame*
>> Was fled, (his glory late, but now his shame:
> For he with spite the gentle boy estranged)
> Now 'long the *Trent* with his new fellows ranged:
>> There *Damon* (friendly *Damon*) met the boy,
>> Where lordly *Trent* kisses the *Darwin* coy,
> Bathing his liquid streams in lovers melting joy.
>
>> (St. 1)

Algon is Phineas' new name; Damon is probably Henry Willoughby; the rivers Trent and Derwin meet in Derbyshire near Risley Hall where Phineas went from Cambridge; and Nicaea, the beloved of Algon, is the Elizabeth Vincent whom Phineas married in 1615. The poem was probably written between 1612 - 14 while Phineas was at Risley and away from Cambridge. Its unique form of dialogue appears related to Phineas' work on his verse drama *Sicelides*, which was presented at King's College, Cambridge, on March 11, 1615: the last half of this eclogue relies heavily upon stichomythia in full and half lines—the same type of dramatic dialogue found in *Sicelides*.[8] The sentiments of the piece, are consistently the old clichés of Courtly Love:

> What ever charms might move a gentle heart,
> I oft have try'd, and shew'd the earnfull smart,
>> Which eats my breast: she laughs at all my pain:
>> Art, prayers, vows, gifts, love, grief, she does
>>> disdain:
>> Grief, love, gifts, vows, prayers, art; ye all are
>>> spent in vain.
>
>> (St. 8).

Although Algon has happily won his Nicaea at the end, the eclogue is not very impressive finally either in originality or in execution.

"The well known fisher-boy" seems more concerned with merely versifying clichés by dexterous flashes of ingenuity than with expressing real feelings.

Eclogue VI, "Thomalin," is also a dialogue about love, this time between Thirsil (the knowing counsellor now) and Thomalin (the love-sick one). Rather conventional, the poem ends with Thirsil's telling Thomalin to turn away from this love to the higher, celestial love of God, and to some "fitting [female] peer."[9] Thomalin apparently took the advice at least in part, for Eclogue VII, "The Prize," is the traditional "singing match" of the pastoral tradition. It pits Thomalin, who is now singing about his new lady-love Stella, against Daphnis (Willoughby?) and his Mira. Thirsil is the judge.

The poem reflects an interesting biographical detail: Thomalin is the "fishers pride / Daphnis the shepherds" and "Thirsil their judge, *who now's a shepherd base,* / But late a fisher-swain, till envious *Chame.* . . . / . . . robb'd . . . him of all his game." Thirsil-Phineas was clearly between worlds. Perhaps the correspondence between the end of the *Piscatorie Eclogues* and of "his game" is only a device for ending the work, but it suggests the end of his whole pastoral-piscatory world and period.

This last eclogue is also the most impressive poetically: the stanzaic patterns are more varied; the verse is consistently better; the style is tighter, crisper, and less adjective-strewn:

> Stella, my starre-like love, my lovely starre:
> Her hair a lovely brown, her forehead high,
> And lovely fair; such her cheeks roses are:
> Lovely her lip, most lovely is her eye:
> And as in each of these all love doth lie;
> So thousand loves within her minde retiring,
> Kindle ten thousand loves with gentle firing.
> Ah let me love my Love, not live in loves admiring!
> (St. 14).

In this stanza, which reflects a clear movement toward direct statement and toward the eschewing of adjectival coloration, the poet's ear is clearly better: the pauses and the word-choices reflect a surer sense of rhythm, a less forced syntax, a more experienced hand. Even the descriptions are more concise and delicate in touch:

> Her naked breast lay open to the spoil;
> The crystal humour trickling down apace,

> Like ropes of pearl, her neck and breast enlace:
> The aire (my rivall aire) did coolly glide
> Through every part: such when my Love I spi'd.
> (St. 10).

Nothing of the apprentice remains in the hand that wrote those lines. The deftness, the lightness, the sure skill, and the loveliness of this eclogue characterize better the poetry to come than most of that of the pastoral period, which the *Piscatorie Eclogues* both illustrate and chronicle.

They also exemplify the age's views on apprenticeship and originality. As a modern scholar has written:

An educated writer of the Renaissance, although he was a man living in his own world, having his own experience, could not simply look in his heart, or around him, and write. He was himself so eagerly responsive to literary tradition, and critical authority was so busy in the necessary task of ordering and refining form and style. . . .[10]

Phineas is a perfect example of that phenomenon.

CHAPTER 6

Phineas Fletcher, Narrative Poet

I Venus and Anchises

A ROUND 1610, during Phineas' pastoral idyll both in Kent, and in Cambridge, he was also writing a sizable body of narrative poetry that included parts of his epic poem *The Purple Island*. These poems not only reveal quite a different aspect of Fletcher's developing talents but also demonstrate how prolific his literary activity was. In fact, his *Venus and Anchises* may be Fletcher's most extraordinary poem in every respect including quality. Although this work was published in 1628 by Thomas Walkley as *Brittain's Ida*, "Written by that Renowned Poet, Edmond Spencer," Spenser's critics have rejected since the eighteenth century Spenser's authorship. Grosart first identified the poem as by Phineas Fletcher in his nineteenth-century edition; and Boas, who devoted six pages in his edition to proving Phineas' authorship, did so with extensive parallel passages from other Fletcher poems. However, the final and conclusive proof was discovered by Ethel Seaton in the 1920s in a manuscript in the Library of Sion College, Cambridge, which contained *Venus and Anchises* and six other poems by Phineas Fletcher.

With some small but important exceptions, this poem was the same as the one published as *Brittain's Ida*. One exception was four additional stanzas. The first two, with which the poem opens, identify the poet as Thirsil, a pastoral poet of Cambridge, who is trying his muse at the request of "fayre Eliza," whose "wishes were his lawes, hir will his fire." The poem is an Ovidian narrative of sensual love that is in the tradition of Shakespeare's *Venus and Adonis* and of Marlowe's *Hero and Leander*. Of the other two stanzas in the manuscript, but omitted from the published version *(Brittain's Ida)*, one is poorly written and redundant (cut out undoubtedly for critical reasons); the other stanza, which describes the climax of the physical consummation of the love of Venus and Anchises, is the most sensual, erotic stanza in the manuscript.

The reasons for this manner of publication are not difficult to deduce. Between 1627 and 1633, under the influence of a new literary patron, Edward Benlowes, Phineas finally had his poetry and prose published, in seven separate volumes. That the Reverend Phineas Fletcher from conservative rural Hilgay, long married and a father, should now not wish to be publicly identified as the author of so sensual a poem as *Venus and Anchises* is understandable. The deleted passages at once tone down the sensuality and remove what was the clear identity of the author by his pen name, Thirsil. The title was changed (the printed one is unrelated to the poem actually), a division into cantos was made, some badly written quatrains were added as arguments (probably by the publisher), a dedication was made to Lady Mary Villiers (a Spenser patroness), and the eulogy on Spenser was affixed to complete the disguise. Although publisher Walkley might have pirated the poem as he did Wither's poems, he had also published some of John Fletcher's plays, and he more likely proved to be for Phineas a convenient collaborator. However Fletcher's poem found its way into print, readers have considerable reason to be thankful; it is extraordinarily good.

The beginning of *Venus and Anchises* evokes the familiar pastoral world of Phineas Fletcher that was discussed in the last chapter:

> Thirsil (poore ladd) whose Muse yet scarcely fledge
> Softlie for feare did learne to sing and pipe,
> And sitting lowe under some Covert hedge
> With Chirping noyse ganne tune his noates unripe,
> Sighing those sighs which sore his heart did gripe,
>   Where lovelie *Came* doeth lose his erring waye
>   While with his bankes the wanton waters playe,
> Which still doe staye behind, yet still doe slippe away;
>
> Thirsil hidde in a willowes shaddowing
> (Nor higher durst his dastard thoughtes aspire)
> Thus ganne to trye his downie Muses wing,
> For soe the fayre *Eliza* deign'd desire
> Hir wishes were his lawes, hir will his fire,
>   And hiding neerer *Came* his stranger name
>   He thought with song his raging fire to tame,
> Fond boye that fewell sought to hide soe great a flame.

Thirsil, the pen name that Phineas had adopted about 1608 at the urging of his Fusca, provides the earliest possible date; the comments about the poem by both Phineas and Giles in *Christ's Victorie and Triumph* establish 1610 as the latest possible date of composition; but the most probable date of composition is 1609. In the prefatory verse that Phineas wrote to *Christ's Victorie* he contrasts Giles' religious verse with the type which composes his own *Venus and Anchises:*

> Fond ladds, that spend so fast your poasting time,
> (Too poasting time, that spends your time as fast)
> To chaunt light toyes, or frame some wanton rime,
> Where idle boyes may glut their lustfull tast,
> Or else with praise to cloath some fleshly slime
> With virgins roses, and faire lillies chast:
> While itching bloods, and youthfull eares adore it.

His declaration that Giles "Hast proov'd the Muses not to Venus bound" seems to refer directly to *Venus and Anchises*. At the end of *Christ's Victorie*, Giles, in contrasting his Muse with that of "Young Thyrsilis," refers to and paraphrases the opening lines (cited above) from *Venus and Anchises:*

> But my greene Muse, hiding her younger head
> Under old Chamus flaggy banks, that spread
> Their willough locks abroad, and all the day
> With their own watry shadowes wanton play,
> Dares not those high amours, and love-sick songs assay.
>   (IV, 50)

Both brothers were highly self-conscious about the poem, but the story of *Venus and Anchises* is both simple and appealing. Among the shepherd boys in Ida Vale before the Greeks attacked Troy was the young, innocent Anchises, "A dainty playfellow for naked love." But his thoughts were neither on the "thousand maidens" who were pursuing him nor on sweet music and delights of song; rather, they were on hunting. One day, while hunting, he chances upon "faire *Venus* grove," a veritable "Garden of delight"; he finds Venus "within halfe naked," asleep. She awakes and thinks him to be her beloved Adonis; but, when she discovers her error, she detains and loves Anchises. He falls in love with her too, but refuses to confess it. Despite the possible danger from jealous Phoebus, she teases Anchises until he confesses his love; and then she rewards him with physical consummation of the love. Foolhardily, he tells the world of the joyful bliss; and, when jealous Jove hears about it, he angrily darts his thunder down upon Anchises, "Blasting his splendent face, and all his beauty swarted."

The structure of the poem is as simple and as straightforward as the narrative. The manuscript version of sixty-one stanzas of eight lines, *ababbccc*, has no subdivisions; but the published version, which as noted, lacks four stanzas, is divided into six cantos, each is headed by a one-quatrain argument. In the narrative itself, characterization is of little importance and is undeveloped. The description, which forms the foundation of the art of this poem, is both the normal, passing kind, which is crisply handled, and the extended word pictures. The most notable examples of the extended pictures are the Garden of Delight (nine stanzas including a love song) and Venus herself (thirteen stanzas). In details, the Garden is similar to Giles' "Garden of Vaine Delight" (*CVT*, II, 39ff), which was influenced by Spenser's Bower of Bliss. Although Venus and her love song resemble Giles' Panglorie (*CVT*, II, 39ff) and Spenser's Acrasia, Phineas' description of Venus renders more systematically the delights of each part of her loveliness and also promotes better an atmosphere of generalized sensuousness:

> Her lips, most happy each in others kisses,
> From their so wisht imbracements seldome parted,
> Yet seem'd to blush at such their wanton blisses;
> But when sweete words their joyning sweet disparted,
> To th' eare a dainty musique they imparted:
>   Upon them fitly sate delightfull smiling,
>   A thousand soules with pleasing stealth beguiling:
>   Ah that such shew's of joyes should be all joyes
>   exiling?
>
>   (Canto 3:6)

Such a tone is ideal for a poem in which atmosphere is more important than character, setting, or plot. It is a technique that both Spenser and Milton used effectively in describing pleasure gardens in narrative poems. Phineas' pacing, which is also a crucial feature of the art in this type of short narrative poem, is excellent; it meanders like a languid stream where lovers might dally.

The basic appeal of the material is the young man's first experience of love and consummation with a beautiful mature lady.

94
GILES AND PHINEAS FLETCHER

The love works within the framework of Courtly Love conventions and sentiments:

> Faire Queene of Love, my life thou maist command,
> Too slender price for all thy former grace,
> Which I receive at thy so bounteous hand;
> But never dare I speake her name and face;
> My life is much lesse-priz'd than her disgrace.
>> (Canto 5:7).

The devotion to beauty, the hyperbole, the delicate tone of "*high amours*" found so often in the poetry of Courtly Love is nicely rendered by Fletcher in the following "confession" of love by Anchises:

> Her forme is as her selfe, perfect Caelestriall,
> No mortall spot her heavenly frame disgraces:
> Beyond compare; such nothing is terrestriall;
> More sweete than thought or pow'rfull wish embraces,
> The map of heaven; the summe of all the Graces.
>> But if you wish more truely limb'd to eye her,
>> Than fainting speech, or words can well descry her,
>> Look in a glasse, & there more perfect you may spy
>>> her.
>> (Canto 5:9).

Nonetheless, the love is basically romantic and sensual—Ovidian. The author invites the reader to delight in the pleasures of first love, which he treats without prudery or prurience; he is frank without ribaldry. Fletcher develops the climax of the poem, the consummation scene, slowly and masterfully:

> And boldned with successe and many graces,
> His hand, chain'd up in feare, he now releast:
> And asking leave, courag'd with her imbraces;
> Againe it prison'd in her tender breast;
> Ah blessed prison! prisners too much blest!
>> There with those sisters long time doth he play;
>> And now full boldly enters loves high way;
>> While downe the pleasant vale, his creeping hand
>>> doth stray.
>> (Canto 6:7).

Throughout, a light almost humorous tone plays about the action, rendering it tasteful as well as delightful, as when "At length into the haven he arrives":

> She not displeased with this his wanton play,
> Hiding his blushing with a sugred kisse;
> With such sweete heat his rudenesse doth allay,
> That now he perfect knowes what ever blisse,
> Elder love taught, and he before did misse:
> That moult with joy, in such untri'd joyes trying,
> He gladly dies; and death new life applying,
>   Gladly againe he dyes, that oft he may be dying.
>   (Canto 6:8)

Of the narrative love poems inspired by Ovid's *Metamorphoses* and *Amores* and written in Renaissance England, Marlowe's *Hero and Leander*, Shakespeare's *Venus and Adonis*, and *The Rape of Lucrece* are probably the best known. However, Thomas Edward's *Narcissus*, Richard Barnfield's *Affectionate Shepherd* and *The Shepherd's Content*, and the anonymous *Salmacis and Hermaphroditus* and *The Scourge of Venus*, are also examples of a type of poem that flourished briefly but heatedly around the turn of the century; and some were probably anonymous for the same reason that Fletcher's was.

Few of these, however, are as good as Fletcher's *Venus and Anchises*, which deserves to be more widely read and known than it is. Unfortunately, the former uncertainty about its authorship and the adulterated version that was published have led to the virtual obscurity of this fine poem. In pace, lightness of touch and taste, overall stylistic qualities, and narrative skill, *Venus and Anchises* is comparable to the best of the tradition—to the Marlowe and Shakespeare poems. In terms of consistency and unity this poem may be Phineas Fletcher's finest work.

II Elisa

The identity of "Eliza," who inspired *Venus and Anchises* and who directed that the poem be written, has intrigued commentators on Fletcher's poetry. The identity is of more than idle curiosity, since his next narrative poem, written shortly after *Venus and Anchises*, was *Elisa*. Although proof of Eliza's identity is lacking,

several likely candidates exist.[1] Phineas' wife Elizabeth seems the
least likely candidate because of the date and the situation which is
described in the poem: the Venus-Anchises relationship is that of a
mature, married woman (with a jealous husband) and a young
bachelor lover. Furthermore, these two lovers of Ida Vale (Brittain's
Ida is Ide Hill in Kent) are separated by a title:

> Nor did she scorne him though not nobly born,
> (Love is nobility) nor could she scorne,
> That with so noble skill her title did adorne.

Since Eliza appears to be a married woman with a title, both
Elizabeth Culpepper, daughter of Lady Culpepper of Kent to
whom Fletcher addressed humorous love poems, and Lady
Elizabeth Irby are the more likely candidates. It was Elizabeth Irby
for whom Fletcher wrote *Elisa, or An Elegie Upon the Unripe
Decease of Sr. Antonie Irby: Composed at the request (and for a
monument) of his surviving Ladie.* Antonie Irby died in 1610 and
the poem appears to have been written then (although it was not
published until 1633).

Elizabeth Irby was born a Peyton of Isleham, which is only nine-
teen miles from Cambridge. Giles, Sr.'s patron had married into
that family, and Robert Peyton, Elizabeth's brother, was a colleague
of Phineas' at King's College. The poem itself indicates that he
knew her well. His cousin Walter Robarts, the center of Phineas'
Kent group, also knew her, as Phineas' verse epistle to Robarts from
Cambridge indicates:

> There would I chant either thy *Gemma's* praise,
> Or els my *Fusca;* (fairest shepherdesse)
> Or when me list my slender pipe to raise,
> Sing of *Eliza's* fixed mournfulnesse,
> And much bewail such wofull heavinesse;
> Whil'st she a dear-lov'd Hart (ah lucklesse!) slew:
> Whose fall she all too late, too soon, too much, did rue.

Most suggestive of all is that he spells her name here with a "z" as
in *Venus and Anchises;* whereas, in *Elisa,* her name is *only* spelled
as in the title. In the next lines of the verse epistle, Phineas laments
being beside the Cam "here among th'unhonour'd willows shade";
in *Venus and Anchises,* "Thirsil hidde in a willowes shaddowing."
But the best evidence for the hypothesis that Elizabeth Irby was the

"Eliza" who inspired both "his fire" and his *Venus and Anchises* is the poem, *Elisa*, itself.

This most assuredly is Phineas Fletcher's strangest poem, as well as his worst; for everything about it seems misguided and difficult to explain. First, the poem is not an "elegy" in the usual literary sense but a narrative poem; second, both the title and the attention are focused not on the dead man but on his wife; third, instead of elegizing the death and providing perspective on it, this poem narrates and dramatizes it and thereby involves the reader in all the emotions of the dying moments; fourth and finally, Elisa's grief, suffering, and sensibilities are what mainly interest Phineas.

The poem is structured in two cantos: the first depicts the deathbed scene; the second follows Elisa from the death to the funeral; and the poet writes as if from firsthand experience. Canto I begins with Irby on his deathbed; "his weeping spouse *Elisa*" is beside him; and, "close by, her sister, fair *Alicia*, sits." Elisa makes a long guilt-ridden prayer (9 - 16), a confession of some "weakness of heart" and of "rebelliousness." When the dying Irby then speaks his "last words" (16 - 40), they form a goodby speech to everything: Alicia and Elisa, the children, God, country, "frail flesh." This address which is rhetorical, sententious, long, and tedious, is filled with hollow, stupid clichés and bathos. Whatever Fletcher may have intended, the effect makes Irby appear to be a self-righteous, sentimental, sententious fool. For example, Irby claims in effect to be a saint:

> I touch the shore, and see my rest preparing
> Oh blessed God! how infinite a blessing
> Is in this thought, that through this troubled faring,
> Through all the faults this guiltie age depressing
>   I guiltlesse past, no helplesse man oppressing;
>   And coming now to thee, lift to the skies
> Unbribed hands, cleans'd heart, and never tainted eyes!
>   (Canto I, 21)

Strangely the description of his death (44 - 50) is, as previously noted, a description of Elisa's suffering and grief.

Canto II starts with a description not only of Elisa's beauty and power to love but of Alicia's great love of Irby (st. 1 - 9). A heavily moralizing and sententious dialogue between the two women commences with Alicia the comforter and Elisa the sufferer (st. 9 - 13). Elisa again expresses guilt and seeks mercy (st. 13 - 20); Alicia

counseles patience and moderation (st. 21 - 23). Alone with the
casket and body, Elisa engages in a long soliloquy (st. 23 - 41) in
which her guilt and her self-vilification dominate her misery and
grief; for she interprets her suffering and her husband's death as
retribution for her sins. Although her crime is not made explicit, she
repeatedly blames her traitorous heart and attacks her body as a
"vile trunk." The allusions to body and bed and some curious sex-
ual imagery leave a strong impression of the kind of "weakness of
heart" to which she is referring. Finally, the pallbearers arrive, they
take Irby away (40 - 41), and the poem ends with more of Elisa's
sufferings, her faintings—and, finally, her sleep.

The poem is uniformly bad. The basic narrative approach to the
death and suffering produces tastelessness, sentimental bathos, and
melodrama. The syntax is often gnarled and confusing; the efforts
at allegory, spotty and awkwardly executed:

> At length lowd Grief thus with a fearfull shriek
> (His trumpet) sounds a battell, joy defying;
> Spreading his colours in *Elisa's* cheek,
> And from her eyes (his watch-tower) farre espying
>   With Hope Delight, and Joy, and Comfort flying,
>   Thus with her tongue their coward flight pursues,
> While sighs, shrieks, tears give chace with never
>   fainting crues:
>   (Canto I, 4)

The tone continually shifts, as above, from the forced sublimity of a
pseudo-epic to colloquial clichés and forced rhymes. The poem is
sophomoric in approach and in conception; the poet is uncomfort-
able and awkward in handling the material. In short, it is a
failure—and a strange failure at that.

III   *An Hypothesis*

In part, the very strangeness of the poem leads to an hypothesis
that seeks to explain the excellence of the first Eliza-inspired
narrative poem and the failure of the second one which followed
close upon it. Eliza Irby may not only have inspired Phineas
Fletcher's love but in the courtly game have also bidden him to
write of love; he may then have produced that stunningly clever little allegory *Venus and Anchises* about lovers like themselves, which

was also a *carpe diem* poem: the final stanza contains the request presented cleverly as the moral of the poem:

> Unworthy he to have so worthy place,
> That cannot hold his peace and blabbing tongue:
>
> . . .
>
> Might I enjoy my love till I unfold it,
> I'de lose all favours when I blabbing told it:
> He is not fit for love, that is not fit to hold it.

When Phineas received her second request for a poem, following the death of her husband, he could neither refuse her nor successfully complete the work because he was too involved with conflicting emotions to deal with the subject effectively. The result reveals, unintentionally, a great deal: the poet's dislike of Irby, his great attraction for Elisa and her beauty, Elisa's guilt and remorse for an illicit love affair, a possible love between Alicia and Irby, and especially Fletcher's anticipation of Elisa's remarriage that is very strangely and awkwardly placed in Irby's dying speech:

> If yet a second *Hymen* do expect thee
> Though well he love thee, once I lov'd as well:
> Yet if his presence make thee lesse respect me,
> Ah do not in my childrens good neglect me.
>
> (Canto I, 38)

It seems likely that Fletcher not only loved her (and may have been her lover) but hoped to marry her. Her wealth, title, and connections with his friends and relatives would have turned his pastoral dream into a brilliant social success. However, in 1614, when Elizabeth Irby married again, it was not to Phineas Fletcher; and his relationship with her may have had something to do with his troubles at Cambridge since he left there in the same year that she remarried. The next year he married another Elizabeth, a commoner from Derbyshire.

IV   Locustae *and* The Locusts or Apollyonists

About 1611, the year of his father's death, Phineas completed a first version of *Locustae vel Pietas Jesuitica*, a narrative poem in

Latin about the gunpowder plot of 1605. Guy Fawkes Day had
already become by act of Parliament "an annual and constant
memorial of that day" in 1605 when Fawkes and at least eight
others had tried to blow up the House of Parliament and King
James. In the universities, poems were composed to celebrate not
only that day but also the deliverance of Protestant England from
Catholic conspirators. Phineas' poem was first dedicated to his
father's friend, James Montagu, Bishop of Bath and Wells; then,
later in the same year, to Prince Henry. After Henry's death in
1612, the poem was expanded, revised, and dedicated to Prince
Charles and his tutor Thomas Murray. In 1627, it was published by
Cambridge printers with a dedication to Giles' old patron, Sir Roger
Townshend. With it was published an English version of the
materials entitled *The Locusts or Apollyonists* which was dedicated
to Lady Townshend. The English poem, customarily referred to as
Apollyonists, is an expanded paraphrastic version of the Latin
poems; but, unlike the Latin, its date or dates of composition are
unknown.[2]

Like Milton's several poems about the same subject, the
Apollyonists presents the gunpowder-Fawkes plot as a "Popish" or
Roman Catholic plot against Protestant England. It originates,
however, with Satan and the forces of hell in their continuous battle
with God. The Christian story of divine history forms the larger
framework, both narrative and theological, of the poem. The poem
thus relates not only to Milton's "In Quintum Novembris" but also
to *Christ's Victorie and Triumph* and *Paradise Lost.* It is an heroic
poem or epyllion of five cantos, 240 stanzas *(ababababccc),* eighteen
hundred lines.

In Canto I, a violent anti-Catholic diatribe (st. 1) and an evoca-
tion of God as Muse and of Rome as the Purple Whore of
Revelations (st. 2 - 4), are followed by the narrative. The action
begins on "a cloudy Night" when "Hels yron gates . . . / Are flung
open" to admit its inhabitants back to an Infernal Council (st. 5 - 9).
"The Porter to th' infernall gate is Sin, / A shapeless shape, a foule
deformed thing"; she has allegorical companions: Despaire,
Sicknes, Languour, Greife (st. 10 - 16). In the middle of the Council
sits "Lordly Lucifer" who is surrounded by the "rebellious Spirits"
who have exchanged "heaven's for hells Sov'raigne." The "Prince
of darkness," described and characterized, rises and delivers a long
speech to the Council (which forms the remainder of the canto [st.
22 - 39]). The earth, claims Satan, unfortunately now lives in peace

and plenty: "Men fearles live in ease, in love, and mirth."
Ignorance, superstition, and war are being supplanted by Truth,
Religion, and Love of Heaven. The center of Satan's problem is
"That little swimming Isle above the rest, / Spight of our spight,"
England; for "God hath fram'd another Paradise" there. This state
of affairs, an anathema to Satan and the forces of Hell, represents
an adverse turn in their continuous struggle against Heaven.

In Canto II, one especially "wily sprite" arises to speak in the
council of Devils after a storm of argument (st. 5). Apollyon or, on
earth, Equivocus is the "father of cheaters" and the "Generall of
those new stamp't Friers," the Jesuits or Apollyonists (st. 6 - 9). In
his long speech to the Parliament of Devils, which comprises the
remainder of the canto (st. 10 - 38) much as Lucifer's speech did in
Canto I, Apollyon declares his unchanging will to continue his part
in the endless war against Heaven with "all the power and wiles
that hell can yeeld". He describes against a background of past
history (one with an obvious anti-Catholic slant) how his troops of
monks and friars, although scattered and weakened by the Reformation, have been reshaped and restrengthened by the Jesuits. In
every "Country, City, Towne," family, and court, these faithful
spies or their agents have been planted; and they are ready to act
"with wicked hand / 'Gainst God and Man . . . To fill th' earth
with sin and blood; heaven with stormes and fright." Equivocus-
Apollyon ends his speech with a call to the devils to go forth to ac-
tivate these Apollyonists in renewed conflict with heaven.

In Canto III, Fletcher, who presents a reading of contemporary
history as the combined work of Jesuits and Devils, depicts the then
contemporary evils in Russia, Poland, Scandinavia, Greece, Spain,
and Rome, "the Purple Whore" (st. 1 - 16). With Rome, Fletcher
describes how the old Roman Empire developed into the Roman
Catholic Empire: "Cesars to chaunge for Friers, a Monarch for a
Monk." What follows is a long, bitterly satiric, anti-Catholic history
of the rise of "Popery" and corruption that presents a wide variety
of specific people, events, rituals, dogmas, and church practices
with elaborate marginal glosses (st. 17 - 40).

In Canto IV, Fletcher describes a conclave at Rome which is inspired and directed by Equivocus but is presided over by Pope Paul
V (st. 1 - 6). Pope Paul makes a speech which reviews church history
and supports the points made in Canto III about specific corrup-
tions (st. 7 - 15). This blatantly anti-Roman Catholic material
presents Paul as an aspiring world tyrant, as "earth God"; and a

speech by Loyola's "eldest Sonne'" continues the review of modern church history in terms of Rome's plans for world domination (st. 18 - 27). A plan is presented to unite France and Spain under Roman control and to destroy "that blessed Isle," England, the chief enemy. The gunpowder plot is to destroy Parliament and King (st. 28 - 37). With joy and glee, the conclave ends (st. 38 - 40).

In Canto V, which describes the plot being carried out, the powder is secreted in the basement of Parliament and is prepared by "firy Faux." However, God sends a warning to his faithful England, a second Israel; the plot is discovered; the agents are apprehended; and England is saved (st. 1 - 17). The remainder of the canto is an encomium that praises God and celebrates His victories and Him as well as England and Prince Charles. The poem ends with a fervent plea to Charles to destroy "that rising Babel seed": Spain, Rome, and Popery ("this second Lucifer").

V *Analysis*

The *Apollyonists* is more distinctly narrative and heroic than *Christ's Victorie*, but both poems use the Christian story of divine history as background and framework. In the *Apollyonists*, the gunpowder plot is another episode in the eternal war between heaven and hell, good and evil, God and Satan, the faithful and the fallen which forms the central conflict in the Christian view of history. The action is presented directly; allegory is rare and decorative rather than central as in parts of *Christ's Victorie* and in most of Spenser's *The Faerie Queene*. This heroic poem is what Milton would call a "brief" epic (like "the book of Job" or his own *Paradise Regained*). Its tone is lofty; its style, epical; its narrative voice, that of the *vates:*

> Teache me thy groome, here dull'd in fenny mire,
> In these sweet layes, oh teach me beare a part:
> Oh thou dread Spirit shed thy heavenly fire,
> Thy holy flame into this frozen heart:
> Teach thou my creeping Muse to heaven aspire,
> Learne my rude brest, learne me that sacred art,
>   Which once thou taught'st thy Israels shepheard-King:
> O raise my soft veine to high thundering;
> Tune thou my lofty song, thy glory would I sing.
>   (V, 18).

Indeed, "decorum" as understood by a Renaissance writer necessitated that a subject dealing with God's "glory" be a "lofty song." Phineas created an appropriate style of "high thundering" much as his brother Giles had—with rhetoric. Canto I is the most notable and distinct in this respect; but, even in it, Phineas in no sense approaches the extremes that characterize Giles' *Christ's Victorie.* (The main features of that style are described at the beginning of Chapter IV.) Phineas too relies on parallelism—varying aspects of isocolon, parison, paromoion—as well as on many figures of speech. Paradox, sententiae, and epic simile appear with particular regularity.

The final alexandrines of each stanza are regularly "rhetorical": "Sleep's but a shorter death, death's but a longer sleep" (I, 6); "In proud, but dangerous gold: in silke, but restless bed" (I, 7); "For her he longs to live, with her he longs to die" (I, 13). These strong last lines also effectively strengthen the prosody. One technique or device of which Phineas seems particularly enamored is the long series or list of details:

> Close by her sat Despaire, sad ghastly Spright,
> With staring lookes, unmoov'd, fast nayl'd to Sinne:
> Her body all of earth, her soule of fright,
> About her thousand deaths, but more within:
> Pale, pined cheeks, black hayre, torne, rudely dight;
> Short breath, long nayles, dull eyes, sharp-pointed
>   chin:
> Light, life, heaven, earth, her selfe, and all shee
>   fled,
> Fayne would she die, but could not: yet halfe dead,
> A breathing corse she seem'd, wrap't up in living lead.
>   (I, 15)

In Phineas' style description, both extended and cursory, works hand in hand with narration to achieve an impressively balanced texture. The long speeches, which comprise a large part of the work, maintain appropriate stylistic decorum. They are often impressive both oratorically and dramatically, as in the following excerpt from Lucifer's speech (I, 31 - 32):

> 31
> But me, oh never let me, Spirits, forget
> That glorious day, when I your standard bore,

And scorning in the second place to sit,
with you assaulted heaven, his yoke forswore.
My dauntlesse heart yet longs to bleed, and swet
In such a fray: the more I burne, the more
    I hate: should he yet offer grace, and ease,
    If subject we are armes, and spight surcease,
Such offer should I hate, and scorne so base a peace.

32

Where are those spirits? Where that haughty rage,
That durst with me invade eternall light?
What? Are our hearts falne too? Droope we with age?
Can we yet fall from hell, and hellish spight?
Can smart our wrath, can griefe our hate asswage?
Dare we with heaven, and not with earth to fight?
    Your armes, allies, your selves as strong as ever,
    Your foes, their weapons, numbers weaker never.
For shame tread downe this earth: what wants but your
    endeavour?

As a speech which simultaneously produces drama and action, con-
vinces as oratory, and reveals and develops character, this one clearly rivals many of Satan's speeches in *Paradise Lost*. And indeed,
Fletcher has developed at least one impressive character in the
poem, one also that influenced Milton's Satan.

Certain other features of this poem that warrant mention include
the strongly nationalistic sentiment that informs the whole work.
The fiercely anti-Catholic bias, one that is totally a product of the
national interpretation of the gunpowder plot, can not be found in
any other Fletcher writing—poetry or prose. History also comprises
a most important part of the work, both the framework of divine,
eternal history and the detailed contemporary history (cantos III
and IV especially). The particular combination of them in the poem
helps also to define the new Baroque heroic poem.[3]

The *Apollyonists* is distinctly not a Spenserian poem; for, rather
than being allegorical, emblematic, and diffuse of episode, it is
directly religious, historical, and tightly structured. In form, art, and
sensibility it moves sharply away from Spenser's *The Faerie Queene*
and strikingly toward Milton's *Paradise Lost*—for which it stands as
a direct, influential precursor.

However, it is not without flaws; its main weaknesses lie in cantos
III and IV in which the review of church and contemporary history
is excessively long and redundant and in which the style too often

becomes journalistic prose in verse form. Although the anti-Catholicism appears only in this poem and was clearly a product of the subject and occasion of the poem, Fletcher's excesses and lapses in taste will seem to be distinct flaws to most readers. Even with these weaknesses, the poem seems more totally successful than *Christ's Victorie.* Phineas demonstrates a more impressive narrative art than his brother, with no less dedication and seriousness of purpose. Phineas' poem, furthermore, seems a more impressive accomplishment with the subject than Milton's "In Quintum Novembris"; and the fact that both John Milton and John Oldham borrowed so much from this poem is itself a considerable testament.[4]

After considering the three narrative poems discussed in this chapter, one must conclude that Phineas, despite one obvious failure, had distinct ability as a narrative poet. He could handle amorous and secular as well as sacred subjects; he found an appropriate style for his story; and he made his story sing as true poetry—an accomplishment which is different and far more difficult than simply versifying a story. Indeed, despite unevenness and failure, these three narrative poems from his late university days reveal a new dimension of his literary ability, accomplishment, and stature.

CHAPTER 7

The Epic and Dramatic Poet

I The Purple Island

SOMETIME about 1606 - 8, Phineas appears to have begun his supremely ambitious literary project, *The Purple Island*. Educated readers, writers, and critics of the Renaissance shared a firm belief that the epic or long heroic poem was inevitably the product of the ripest years and of the maturest abilities. The epic, which was held to be the most difficult and demanding type of poetry, represented the epitome of literary art. It had formed, for example, the final and crowning achievement in the literary careers of the greatest poets, ancient and modern: Homer, Vergil, Spenser, Tasso, Ariosto, and Du Bartas for example.

For a young novice-poet, still a "prentice," to undertake and produce an epic poem was unprecedented. Phineas' decision to do so reveals just how young and fanciful his daydreams could be in the period of his pastoral-literary idyll; it reveals also how profound was his commitment to literature. From what has been said previously about these years, his design of combining pastoral and heroic modes in a long narrative poem should seem at least understandable—as understandable as that "The Kentish lad that lately taught / His oaten reed the trumpets silver sound, / Young Thirsilis" should be Narrator and that Phineas' beloved Kentish crew should be included as characters. By 1610, when Giles, Jr. described his brother's work in progress, the main design and some parts, including the final scene of the finished epic, had been written. Internal evidence, including topical references and stylistic features, indicates, however, that the poem continued to be worked upon until publication in 1633.

The subject of *The Purple Island* is man himself. However, as the title suggests, man is treated allegorically as an Island: "An Isle I fain would sing, an Island fair" (I, 34). By the end of the poem, the

106

Island has become also a metaphor, a figure, and a complex symbol for man. The pastoral world forms only an external structural framework: one of the shepherd crew, Thirsil (Phineas' pseudonym from about 1606 - 15), narrates the contents of each of the twelve cantos to the other shepherds. Thirsil is a shepherd in both senses of pastoral: classical and Christian. How closely the two worlds operate in the Renaissance generally and in the poem specifically is illustrated in Thirsil's initial invocation:

> Great Prince of Shepherds, thou who late didst deigne
> To lodge thy self within this wretched breast,
> (Most wretched breast such guest to entertain,
> Yet oh most happy lodge in such a guest!)
>   Thou first and last, inspire thy sacred skill;
>   Guide thou my hand, grace thou my artlesse quill:
> So shall I first begin, so last shall end my will.
>   (I, 33)

The voices of the *vates*—literally a poet-priest before the poem was completed—that is singing "Sacred Song" is as unmistakable in *The Purple Island* as it was in its "sister Muse," *Christ's Victorie and Triumph*. Phineas' poem, characteristically, is much larger and more ambitious than Giles; for it has five thousand lines in seven-line stanzas, *ababccc*. Like the epics of his mentors Vergil and Spenser (and later Milton), Phineas' epic has twelve parts (cantos).

Although the design contains many substructures and very diverse kinds of material, at least two large outlines can be discerned. First, the work covers three large areas: the external, physical anatomy of Man the Island; the internal, moral-mental-spiritual anatomy of Man-Island; and the war of virtues and vices in the Man-Island. Second, the Christian story of divine history forms an important unifying aspect of this work as it did for the *Apollyonists* and for *Christ's Victorie and Triumph*. The history of the conflict between God and Satan over man, which is woven throughout the work, provides a background against which the details of the Man-Island allegory can be extensively developed. Furthermore, that conflict and the struggle provide the only plot and action in the work. The Christian story provides, in short, something of a "higher Argument" for the whole epic.

II   The Purple Island: *Synopsis by Cantos*

Canto I, which forms an Introduction or Proem, establishes the subject, the type of poem, the literary precedents (both pastoral and heroic), and the biographical and religious dimensions. The poem opens in a pastoral world of Spring, flowers, and "shepherd-boyes, who with the Muses dwell . . . by . . . learned *Chame*." Biographical details about Phineas, Giles, and the Cambridge-Kent crew follow (3 - 9), Thirsil (Phineas), nominated by the pastoral crew as "lord of them, and of their art," is asked to sing; and his song comprises the rest of the poem. The Muses are invoked, they are questioned about appropriate subjects of heroic verse, and they are asked "What now remains unthought on by those Sages, / Where a new Muse may trie her pineon? / What lightning Heroes" can be found? (9). There follows a review of great subjects and works, ancient and modern, by Homer, Vergil, the Greek tragedians, Ovid, Sanazaro, and Du Bartas (9 - 16). This review ends in a contrast of the honors given these poets by their ages with the abuse and neglect given poets by the present "witless vulgar . . . throng." More biographical musings follow (17 - 31) about false worldly success and about the beauty of Thirsil's (Phineas') own quiet rural, pastoral life with wife and child (after 1623), where "singing might I live, and singing die!" without the need of patrons.

An invocation and a prayer to the "Great Prince of shepherds," Christ, and an apostrophe on sacred poetry follow (32 - 3), then the poet announces the subject: "An Isle I fain would sing, an Island fair" (34). The Purple Island-Man is then related to various episodes and aspects of the Christian story of divine history: the creation of man and the world, the temptation of man by Satan, man's fall, and his promised redemption from death by Christ (35 - 59). The canto concludes with Thirsil's questioning of his own maturity for so ambitious an effort as an heroic poem ("My callow wing, that newly left the nest / How can it make so high a towering flight?") and his wondering if Giles' poem will outstrip his ("my sister Muse, mayst well go higher"). The shepherds retire from the noonday sun "into the glade" (59 - 60), and the canto ends.

Canto II, like all cantos in the poem, begins in the pastoral mode: "*Thirsil* on a gentle rising hill" amidst his flock and "circled with a lovely crue / Of Nymphs & shepherd-boyes . . . his song renew." The narrative starts with the effects of the fall upon man, "that

glorious image" of Christ (2 - 4); and this discussion leads to the extended physical description of man's anatomy that comprises the
rest of this canto (5ff). To help keep clear the relation between the
human anatomy and the topography of an Island, Fletcher glosses
long, detailed anatomical descriptions in the margins. He begins
with the "foundation": "bones and cartilage" (rock and earth),
blood, veins, arteries, nerves (streams, rivers, fountains, trenches).
(5 - 13).

The Island of Man is divided into three "Metropolies" or gover-
ning regions (Belly, Brest, and Head) which serve as the main
anatomical subdivision of man for the remainder of poem. The rest
of the canto is given to a detailed anatomy of the Belly or stomach.
Some of the main features described are the muscles (walls and
guards), skin (fences), fat (rampier), peritonaeum (gate), Urine-
lake, liver, gall, spleen, kidneys, guts (six lesser cities and suburbs
which are each named Koilia, Cephal, Hepar, etc., and described in
appropriately metaphoric or allegorical terms [14 - 46]). The canto
ends at sundown with the "crew" retiring, but anticipating
"Tomorrow with the day [when] we may renew our song."

Canto III commences with Thirsil's apology to his crew for "my
rudeness all unfit / To frame this curious Isle, whose framing
yet / Was never thoroughly know to any human wit"; he invokes
again the divine aid of "Thou Shepherd-God" (1 - 4). He then continues his anatomical description of the Belly where he left off in
Canto II with "Th' Arch-citie *Hepar*," the liver. He describes in
terms of Island topography numerous aspects of the liver, the
spleen, the kidneys, the ureter, and of the generative organs, which
are treated with great modesty—"Flie then those parts, which best
are undescri'd"—and moralizing (5 - 29). There follows a strangely
extraneous encomium on Queen Elizabeth and Essex and an attack
on her Spanish Catholic detractors (30 - 34), but this section may
have been included either to lengthen a short canto or to support
his suggestion that the poem was composed in his "raw youth."

In Canto IV, Thirsil's song moves to "th' Isles Heart-Citie" and
describes in great detail ribs, breast, muscles of respiration,
diaphragm, lungs (including larynx, epiglottis, cartilage), and the
heart (1 - 33). In Canto V, the Head is anatomized: "divided into
the Citie, and suburbs; the brain within the wall of the skull, and
the face without." Since the Head (Thelu) is "most like to heaven
. . . being highest in this little world" (man as microcosm), Thirsil
must invoke again "heav'nly fire" to complete the seventy-one

stanzas of detailed Head-topography that are replete with classical mythology.

Canto VI, which represents a somewhat different emphasis and direction from the preceding one, was almost surely the first part that Phineas wrote (about 1606 - 8).[1] Thenot suggests the new subject:

> We long to know that Islands happy nation:
> Oh! do not leave thy Isle unpeopled here.
> Tell us who brought, and wherce these colonies;
> Who is their King, what foes, and what allies;
> What laws maintain their peace, what warres & victories
> (VI, 3).

Thirsil begins his long description of the *internal anatomy* of the Man-Island with Adam and Eve ("those Heroes, who in better times / This happy Island first inhabited / In joy and peace"); he then moves to the fall of man and the entry to the Isle of that "false, foul, fiend-like companie" of Satan (7 - 11). In heaven a debate between Justice and Mercy takes place (12 - 20) just as in *Christ's Victorie and Triumph* (mentioned twice by name). The effects of the fall are suggested—"th' Isle is doubly rent with endless warre and fright—in terms of ancient and modern history (20 - 8).

Then begins the *mental-moral anatomy* of the Isle of man (28); for "The Islands Prince . . . th' all-seeing *Intellect*," God's "Viceroy here," is beset in his tower by enemies from hell (28 - 40). He has as "Counsellers" the five senses and "three pillars of state"—Fancie, Understanding, Common Sense (41 - 51); his Queen, Will, is attended by Conscience (52 - 70). The canto ends with an encomium to the Son of God (71 - 77), "immortal redeemer," Man's hope.

In Canto VII, Thirsil's song commences with a moral-religious theme: happiness and success are not to be found on earth (1 - 3). A review of fallen empires—Syria, Persia, Rome, Turkey (4 - 8)—evidences this fact. The reason is that some disdained the "great Lords . . . royall service . . so down were flung. . . . In heav'n they scorn'd to serve, so now in hell they reigne." Their "Prince a Dragon, swoln with pride and hate," tempts men "to lust and pride." The rest of the canto presents Satan's companions and qualities as allegorical personifications: the Flesh (Caro), Adultery (Moechus), Jealousie, Fornication, Sodomie, Lasciviousnesse, Idolatrie, Witchcraft, Heresie, Hypocrisie, Superstition, Hatred,

Variance, Emulation, Wrath, Strife, Sedition, Murder, Drunkennesse, and more (14 - 85). These portraits of the sins of the world are luridly descriptive in the fashion of late Medieval and early Renaissance theological allegory.

In Canto VIII which is basically a continuation of Canto VII, Cosmos, the son of Satan, represents "the world or Mammon." His companions of battle are presented and described, as in VII, as allegorical personages; they are moral or ethical "Vices": Fearfulness, Foolhardiness, Arrogance, Prodigalitie, Covetousness, Feeblemindedness, Ambition, Flatterie, Baseness of minde, Morositie, Mad Laughter, Rusticitie, Impudence, and so forth. (Aristotle's *Ethics* is regularly glossed.) These Vices are also Knights who are prepared for battle.

Canto IX consists of another series of allegorical portraits, the Virtues: Spiritto and Urania (heaven), Knowledge, Contemplation, Care, Humilitie, Obedience, Faith, Meditation, Penitence, Hope, Promise, Love, Remembrance, and Gratitude; also "A lovely Swain . . . *Loves* twin" (the Son of God) is described at length (37 - 50). In Canto X Thirsil switches from theological Virtues to moral-ethical ones such as Peaceablenesse, Fortitude, Long Suffering, Courtesie, Temperance, Chastitie (described at length as "*Parthenia*," 24 - 40), and Modestie (42 - 43).

Canto XI moves to warfare action. The "mighty Heroes [Virtues] . . . Glitt'ring in arms . . . Stood at the Castle (3) gate, now ready bent To sally out, and meet the enemies [Vices]." The Island King, "Intellect," his wife "Volleta," and their Daughter "*Eclecta*"—the Beloved or Intended of Love (God)—lead them to battle (4 - 15). The Knight, Chastitie, unmounts Porneios in single combat (16 - 25). The "subtil Dragon" disguises "false Delight" as "true Delight" and sends him for a sneak attack on Chastitie (26). When False Delight is wounded, she calls upon the aid of "high Love," who sends help to save her (28 - 39). The Dragon, vexed, sends out bands of skirmishing knights who fight against the Virtue-Knights with poisoned weapons and cunning tricks and slights (40 - 49). By the end of the day, the Knight-Virtues retire "neare to fainting" and "opprest with wounds" (50).

Canto XII opens with a lengthy autobiographical panegyric about the good life of the rural shepherd in contrast to court life (1 - 8). Thirsil returns to "singing of thy warres and dreadfull fight" and narrates a full-blown war in heroic terms (9 - 67). Faith and Knowledge lead the battle against the Vice-Knights, they reap havoc and destruction upon them (12 - 19). When the Dragon, sens-

ing reversal, spews forth "Black smothering" vapors of Chaos and
Night to protect his "bat-eyed legions" (20 - 24), Faith's diamond
shield foils the plan with blazing light. The Dragon vomits up his
most loathsome crew: Hamartia (Sin), Despair, and Death—all
deformed Serpentine monsters (26 - 39), the sight of whom
paralyzes the Virtues, allowing the Dragon to bind them. Fair
"Eclecta," grief stricken, Prays to her "dearest Lord," and the
Thunderer, "Like a Thousand Sunnes," comes out to battle, blasts
the Dragon, and ends the war (54 - 65). The Dragon is imprisoned;
the Prince of the Isle comes out of the castle to "meet the Victour"
(66 - 8); the Love and Hymen of God and Eclecta are celebrated
(69 - 87). Thirsil ends his song and is led home by "the lovely
Nymphs with garlands new / His locks in Bay and honour'd Palm-
tree bound" (88 - 9).

III   The Purple Island: *Commentary*

The Purple Island qualifies easily as one of the most unusual
poems in English: the work may be also the most eclectic in design
and the most uneven in performance. The pastoralism, for example,
is essentially external and very superficial, and its presence in the
poem seems mostly owing to Fletcher's preoccupation with
pastoralism during the period when the poem was conceived and
begun.

Phineas' mentors during this period, Vergil and Spenser, receive
full credit: of the four statements of his debt to the two literary
giants, three occur in this poem. The following stanza illustrates the
intensity of his admiration as well as his awareness of the progres-
sion from pastoral to heroic in both their work and his:

> Two shepherds most I love with just adoring;
> That *Mantuan* swain, who chang'd his slender reed
> To trumpets martiall voice, and warres loud roaring,
> From *Corydon* to *Turnus* derring-deed;
> And next our home-bred *Colins* sweetest firing;
> Their steps not following close, but farre admiring:
> To lackey one of these is all my prides aspiring.
> (VI, 5).

Phineas did not so much change his "reed to trumpet" as play both
instruments together. The influence of Spenser appears greater,

because of the allegory, but Vergil is always mentioned first by Phineas. Like Giles, Phineas also acknowledged the influence of Du Bartas and Sanazaro.

Giles' *Christ's Victorie and Triumph* is itself also an acknowledged influence. In fact, the two brothers were writing these two long poems at the same time; the two poems seem "from self-same fountain [to] flow"; and, in important respects, they seem "two joyn'd in one, or one disjoyn'd in two" (PI, I, 3). For example, the sense of the poet as *vates* singing "Sacred Song" appears equally strong in both poems.[2] Moreover, the Christian story of divine history provides the continuity, background, frame of reference, and significance, of both poems. This resemblance, together with the type and number of cross-references to each others' poem, indicates that the two brothers were working closely together during these years. They even may have been consciously writing their poems as a joint or related project that was perhaps to be a single work.[3]

Whether such an exact plan ever existed, the two works certainly share another obvious feature, allegory. Three writers explicitly mentioned by Giles in "To the Reader"—Spenser, Du Bartas, and Prudentius—use allegory in the same way that Phineas does in *The Purple Island*. The allegorical war of Virtues and Vices within man, made famous by Prudentius' *Psychomachia*, appears in both *The Faerie Queene* and *The Purple Island;* and in all three works it serves a similar moral, ethical, and theological purpose.[4]

The physiological or anatomical allegory, physical man as a purple island (II - V), is, however, something quite different. This use makes the poem read like science turned into literature and forms an almost separate (and separable) section. The long, involved marginal glosses make clear that Fletcher had studied human anatomy or physiology. A. B. Langdale, who investigated the source of Phineas' knowledge, concludes in *Phineas Fletcher, Man of Letters, Science, and Divinity* (New York, 1937), that Phineas had not only studied the major ancient and Renaissance works but had witnessed human dissections: "Parts of his information seem to have come from Aristotle, Galen, and Greece; from Ingrassias, Italy, and the sixteenth century; from Vicary; from John Caius and Gonville and Caius dissectors; but the intrinsic core was the product of no book, ancient or modern, nor of hearsay. Nothing intervened between the cadaver and the poet, and his writing was a reporting of what he had seen with his own eyes" (p. 208).

IV   The Purple Island: *Criticism*

Langdale takes the unique critical position that the scientific part
(II - V) forms, in fact, the most valuable part of the poem as well as
of Phineas' whole career: "These cantos are the climax of the poetry
and the life of Phineas Fletcher. They rescue him from the slough of
the commonplace and set him upon the high plain where he walks,
humbly as was his wont, with Sir Francis Bacon, Galileo Galilei,
William Harvey, and the other soldiers of science who warred
against holy edicts, superstitions, lethargies, and all that vagrant
rout" (p. 209). Since the four cantos in question are the sole example of either special "scientific" knowledge or scientific emphasis in
Phineas' work, Langdale's inclusion of him among the "soldiers of
science" (not to mention among that august group) seems quixotic.
Furthermore, science is one thing; literature, another. These cantos,
besides demonstrating just how incompatible the two can be, also
reflect staggering esthetic and literary problems.
    The first major problem is that the primary effects and purposes
of this section are not literary; they are scientific. Anatomy or
physiology in verse form is still anatomy or physiology. And what
Phineas gives his readers is essentially an extended anatomy lesson
in verse form. But verse is not poetry, although Fletcher tried to
achieve both. One reason he did not, however, is due to the
problem of language that he encountered and could not solve. To
translate anatomical language into common layman's terms is difficult enough, but to turn a technical vocabulary into poetry involves more: translating a highly precise but denotatively limited
vocabulary into its opposite. For Fletcher, the problem was even
greater: he had to translate anatomy (the Body) into a combination
of geographical jargon (the Island) and esthetic language (poetry).
The result generally and in *The Purple Island* specifically is large-
scale incomprehensibility. Without the aid of detailed anatomic
glosses, the reader of the following example finds the content
obscure and unclear, both as anatomy and as geography:

> Much like a mount it easily ascendeth;
> The upper part's all smooth as slipperie glasse:
> But on the lower many a cragge dependeth;
> Like to the hangings of some rockie masse:
>   Here first the purple fountain making vent.
>   By thousand rivers through the Isle dispent,
> Gives every part fit growth and daily nourishment.

Only the marginal gloss makes this passage meaningful: "The livers upper part rises & swells gently; is very smooth, and even; the lower in the outside like to an hollow rock, rugged & craggy. From it rise all the springs of bloud, which runnes in the veins" (III, 7).

Without such gloss, most of the content is meaningless. With the gloss, however, the text must be read like a translation: from gloss to stanza, from gloss to stanza; and this procedure makes it impossible to read the poem straight through as a poem. Worse, it forces the reader to jump back and forth from the world and language of anatomy to those of geography and poetry. The process is fatiguing, unpleasant, and unrewarding. Most of the time the reader is more aware of the process of translation than of the subject.

Fletcher's decision to try to combine science and literature in this fashion was a serious error in artistic and esthetic judgment. That whole section of the poem (II - V) is dull, distasteful, static, and misguided because it is basically extraneous to the rest of the poem, since the parts of the body actually play no direct role in the poem's conflict and warfare (VI - XII). This error in judgment also increases dramatically the eclectic nature of the work. However, unlike eclectic masterpieces by Spenser and Milton, the parts of *The Purple Island* are dissonant. The blood and organs of the anatomy theater ill become the shepherds, the flocks, and the rural "ditties" of the pastoral idyll. Both contrast with the heroic, valorous combat of Medieval Knights who are personified Virtues and Vices, or with the Christian mythological devils and angels. The pipes of peace ill support the trumpets of war. Finally, the science lessons (II - V), the interminable gallery of allegorical portraits (VI - X), and the epic battles (XI - XII) never coalesce.

It is not surprising, therefore, that this poem has been almost universally disliked by critics. A recent review of criticism about this poem over the centuries concluded that it was considered "a curiosity, a literary eccentric to be exclaimed about, deplored, or chuckled at as the spirit moves."[5] Most critics have found the poem "bizarre," "strange," "ugly and arid," "fantastic," or worse. George MacDonald, for example, exclaimed, "Of all the strange poems in existence, surely this is the strangest!" And E. Sanford, comparing the Fletcher brothers' poems, wrote that "Phineas, with a livelier fancy, had a worse taste. He lavished on a bad subject the graces and ingenuity that would have made a fine poem on a good design." Just as correct as Sanford's view is the comment of H. Headley, the eighteenth-century Fletcher apologist, about the first

five cantos of the poem: "in the course of which the reader forgets
the poet, and is sickened with the anatomist. Such minute attention
to this part of the subject was a material error in judgment; for
which, however, *ample amends* are made in what follows."[6]

Unfortunately but understandably, most critics and readers seem
not to proceed beyond the objectionable section of the poem.
However, Headley is quite correct; for the remainder of the poem is
much stronger, more consistent, and much more impressive. Since
cantos VI - XII taken alone form a whole and integral poem, the
anatomical cantos, which can be seen as a separate and separable
section of the poem, may not have been part of the original design
but have been added later (around 1614 - 15) when Phineas returned briefly to Cambridge. Perhaps he was exploring medicine as
a possible way to remain at Cambridge. More likely, these
anatomical verses may have been written to impress the famous
science-minded Lord Francis Bacon, Giles' patron. Perhaps they
were meant to round out the work to twelve cantos. At any event,
the "science" section (II - V), as almost all the criticism reveals, is
the single main reason for the poem's failure. After such mitigating
circumstances as youth, naiveté, and immature judgment have been
considered, the critic still places around the author's neck the
albatross of an instructive but monumental failure.

V   Sicelides, *A Piscatory*

As a dramatist, Phineas wrote better but achieved less attention
than as an epic poet; and his play *Sicelides* may represent his last
major effort to achieve worldly success through literature. As
previously noted, Fletcher suddenly returned on December 16,
1614, to residence at King's College where he remained until March
25, 1615, when he departed forever. This three-month return was
related to the Royal Visit of King James to Cambridge on March 7 -
11. The festivities that surrounded the visitation of the King and his
company, which included Prince Charles (to whom *Locustae* had
been dedicated) and John Donne, involved debates, disputations,
feastings, and plays provided by select colleges. King's College had
the honor of presenting the final play on the last evening for an
audience of perhaps some two thousand persons, including eminent
representatives of academe, church, and state. Since that final play
was *Sicelides* by Phineas Fletcher, its presentation would surely
have been Phineas' grandest moment of recognition if the King and

his whole party had not been forced to return unexpectedly to London on the morning of March 11. If the play was not performed as scheduled on that evening, the audience for whom it was intended missed an evening of theater and a fine, professional piece of dramatic writing.

VI   Sicelides: *Synopsis*

The play commences with a Prologue spoken by "*Chamus*" that invokes a Royal Muse; begs consideration for the "infancy" of actors and playwright; and compares England and Sicily, the setting of the play and source of the title. In Act I, scene i, one of the two principal young romantic leads, Perindus, converses with a friend just returned home from war; and, during this conversation, a group enters comprised of a chorus of priests and fishers; Olinda, his sister; and Glaucilla, the sister of Thanlander, his best friend. In the course of scenes ii - iv, the romantic situation is unveiled: Perindus loves Thanlander's sister, Glaucilla; Thanlander, in turn, loves Perindus' sister, Olinda. Olinda, however, has been tricked by an enchanter, Mago (Archimago) into believing Thanlander is dead and has fallen into his clutches. The exposition of plot and situation moves slowly through excessively long, "poetic" speeches. The piscatory paraphernalia offers no special symbolic enrichment of the conventional pastoral world which the play manifests. The play is basically high romantic comedy.

Act II, Scene i, introduces another and lower level of action and comedy with the wise and witty Conchylio, servant to Cosma (a lovely lady of loose morals), and Pas, a fool in love with Cosma ("Ah Pas, asse, passing asse"). Fredocaldo, an old dotard who is also in love with Cosma, adds further spice as the January lover. These three—the clever servant, the fool, and the January lover—provide another comic dimension as well as another love plot. Still a third level of comedy is provided by two foolish servants, Cancrone and Scrocca, whose actions and words form the lowest of comedy: slapstick, puns, jest, foolish nonsense. In Act II, Olinda is saved from the monster Mago by one Atycles whom she marries in gratitude.

In Act III, Perindus and Glaucilla engage in a Courtly Love battle of the sexes: "My love, my hate, my joy, my miserie!" Perindus is avoiding his true love, Glaucilla, because of a danger the oracle had forecast. Olinda, growing more enamored of the memory of

Thanlander, has grown cold to Atycles. Pas and Fredocaldo continue to struggle for the favors of Cosma, but the tricks and games of Conchylio keep them, as well as Cancrone and Scrocca, on a wildly comic, ribald merry-go-round.

Act IV additionally complicates the lives and relationships of the three groups of lovers in terms of high, middle, and low comedy. The act moves quickly and lightly through six scenes of love intrigue and plotting—scenes which highlight a cyclops, disguises, and a variety of comic situations. Conchylio, the principal plotter, disguises as Cosma and engages in a series of love scenes in the forest with Pas, Fredocaldo, Cancrone, and even the cyclops. These forest scenes are not unlike those in Shakespeare's *A Midsummer Night's Dream*. The pace is swift; the atmosphere is gay, witty, bawdy, lighthearted; the act is full of slapstick, puns, jests, and good situational comedy of a sophisticated and earthy type.

In Act V, through the plotting of Mago and Cosma, Olinda appears to have been killed; Glaucilla is to be executed for the crime—along with Cancrone and Scrocca for their negligence. However, Atycles (Thanlander in disguise) and Olinda discover their true love. The *deus ex machina* entrance of Tyrinthus, father of Perindus and Olinda, imprisoned by pirates for twenty years but now escaped, sets all lovers aright. The play ends with a happy hymen song for the romantic lovers; Cosma and Cancrone go off to bed; and an epilogue bids "pleasure" to the audience.

VII   Sicelides: *Commentary and Criticism*

Despite the rather academic sound of its title, *Sicelides* bears a clear relationship to the Elizabethan and Jacobean stage, both private and public. The first impression that the play may produce is to remind one of the theater world of the University Wits of the 1570s and 1580s: a world of pastoral dramas and private performances at the universities; a theatrical world in which the idealized types from the pastoral world of books mixed with low-life realism and with real audiences. It was a combination which spread to the public stage and never entirely left it. For pastoral romance, Sidney's *Arcadia* was of course seminal both on and off the stage; but there were also plays: Peele's *Arraignment of Paris* and *The Old Wives' Tale*, Greene's *Friar Bacon and Friar Bungay*, Shakespeare's *Love's Labors Lost*, and Lyly's *Alexander and Campaspe* and his *Endimion*. Indeed, *Endimion* bears a particular likeness to

Sicelides. Both, for example, deal with love in important thematic ways; both present three groups of lovers from three different worlds of love (although Lyly relates his more directly to levels on the platonic leader of love and to court personages); and both deal simultaneously with idealized love sentiments (romance), romantic infatuation, and ribald low comedy. Phineas' father, Giles, Sr., probably knew Lyly at court; and Phineas could easily have seen a performance of *Endimion* in London or at Cambridge.

Multiple plots like those of *Sicelides* remain an earmark of Elizabethan and Jacobean dramas. And high romantic comedy, which was often tinged or infused with pastoralism, which mixed middle-class and low-life social types, which intermixed verse and prose, and which used far-away settings and farce, was almost a formula for Shakespeare and his contemporaries. Piscatory remained an unusual variation of pastoral, but this kind of pastoral romance or high romantic comedy that was popular in the 1580s had a notable revival around 1605 - 15, as is witnessed, for example, by Shakespeare's *Pericles, Cymbeline, The Winter's Tale,* and *The Tempest* or by cousin John Fletcher's *The Faithful Shepherdess* and (with Beaumont) *Philaster.*

Measured against this background, it would be difficult to determine whether Phineas was returning to an older type of play, popular in his youth, or was trying to place himself in 1614 among the most fashionable, leading lights of the London theater. In either event, the play works with the known conventions and ingredients of theater history of 1575 - 1615, in which the plays put on at the universities, at inns-of-court, at the court itself, and upon the great London public stages can not be always clearly distinguished. Furthermore, *Sicelides* was written for an educated, worldly audience; for the wit, humor, and puns are consistently sophisticated, urbane, racy.

The play is not, however, without weaknesses. The dialogues, especially those in Act I, tend to be overly rhetorical, long, and self-consciously stylized. There is little interesting character development or characterization. The characters are, in fact, all recognizable Elizabethan types: the wily servant, the nondescript, romantic leads, even a Calaban creature (Orke). Since most Elizabethan-Jacobean drama was eclectic, *Sicelides* is no exception; furthermore, little seems in any way original or unusual. In fact, except for the piscatory paraphernalia, the play seems like another good, solid example of one recurrent type of Elizabethan-Jacobean play. It has some very good low-comedy scenes and, overall, can easily be rated as a more than competent piece of stagecraft.

In terms of Phineas' own work, the play offers further evidence of the growing diversity and breadth of Phineas' talents and accomplishments. Like *Venus and Anchises*, *Sicelides* was also published anonymously. One can only wonder, as Phineas himself must have done thereafter, what direction his career and writing might have taken had King James, Prince Charles, and the royal company remained as planned in Cambridge through the evening of March 11, 1615, and witnessed the performance of *Sicelides*.

CHAPTER 8

Phineas Fletcher: The Ripe Years, 1615 - 35

I *"Our ripest hopes hung blossomed"*

ALTHOUGH Phineas at the time viewed his departure from Cambridge in extremely negative terms, that event of 1615 clearly formed a major watershed in his life, career, and literature. Either around 1612 or after the *Sicelides* disappointment (1615), he wrote a verse epistle to his dear friend John Tomkins that described the departure:

> Since then to other streams I must betake me,
> And spitefull *Chame* of all ha's quite bereft me;
> Since Muses selves (false Muses) will forsake me,
> And but this *Nothing*, nothing els is left me;
> Take thou my love, and keep it still in store;
> That given, *Nothing* now remaineth more.
>
> ("To Thomalin")

Phineas clearly did undergo an almost total change in ambience and in life-styles in 1615 when he was midway through his life at the age of thirty-three. Cambridge and Kent had comprised his whole social, economic, and literary world. They had formed the nucleus of his hopes and aspirations as well as the source of his poetic subjects and inspiration. To exchange all that for a poor chaplaincy in the country home of farming gentry in a remote area of Derbyshire, far from Cambridge and farther from Kent, represented a reversal of fortune—if not a trauma. Whatever the quiet joys of Risley Hall and the congeniality of the Willoughbys, Phineas was isolated from his literary world and was living among farmers. Perhaps to compensate, he married Elizabeth Vincent in that year, or early in the next one. They started a family: eight children were born to them over the next twenty years. In 1621, Phineas was given the recently vacated rectorship at Hilgay, Norfolk, a living owned by Willoughby; he spent the remainder of his life performing the duties of the rector at Hilgay.

Furthermore, however negative he may once have seemed about his post-Cambridge prospects, clearly he adjusted to his new situation. And, rather than ending his relationship with the Muses, his departure marked only a new phase and direction of that relationship. The next fifteen to twenty years of his life, from about 1615 to 1635, reveal a literary activity and productivity that exceeded even his remarkably prolific Cambridge years.[1]

For one thing, he continued work on his epic *The Purple Island* as well as upon his epyllion, *Locustae* or *Apollyonists*. For another, he continued to write short poems; in fact, he produced a sizable body of quite varied and generally impressive short poems which are discussed at length in this chapter. In addition, he wrote and published two religious books: *The Way to Blessedness, A Treatise or Commentary on the First Psalm* (1632) which was dedicated to his patron, Sir Henry Willoughby, Baronet, and *Joy in Tribulation, or Consolations for Afflicted Spirits* (1632), a general religious work of 339 pages, which was dedicated to "His most Honorable Cousin, Sir Walter Robarts, Knight and Baronet and his Gracious Lady," of Kent, for whose marriage many years before he had written "An Hymen." Perhaps he also worked upon *A Father's Testament*, a third long book of religious prose, which was published posthumously in 1670.[2]

The move to Hilgay, Norfolk, in 1621 must have proved both desirable and beneficial for Fletcher since his residence was only twenty some miles from Cambridge and was even closer to the larger cities of Ely and King's Lynn. Moreover, this location was closer to Alderton, Suffolk, where Giles was performing his duties as rector; and, with Phineas' patron residing still in Derbyshire, he surely had much greater freedom as well as responsibility.

During the decade of the 1620s, a new group of literary friends and acquaintances appear in his life. Francis Quarles, whom Phineas seems to have met at Cambridge during residence there, apparently visited him rather frequently during that decade and encouraged his poetry. Not only did Quarles write some glowing dedicatory verse to Phineas' *The Purple Island* in which he called him "The Spencer [sic] of this age" but he included in his own *Emblems* (1635) the figure of a globe on which were inscribed only four place names, and Phineas' Hilgay was one of them. Izaak

Walton, the biographer of Donne, and Herbert also knew Phineas (although perhaps not until the 1630s) and wrote of him in *The Complete Angler* (1653): "Phineas Fletcher, an excellent divine, and an excellent angler; and the author of excellent Piscatory Eclogues, in which you shall see the picture of this good man's mind: and I wish mine to be like it" (175 - 6).

Other acquaintances who can be definitely related to Phineas' poetry during the 1620s include John Arrowsmith, rector at St. Nicholas chapel, King's Lynn, who wrote dedicatory verse for *The Purple Island* and who later became master of Trinity College, Cambridge; Dr. Daniel Fairclough ("Featley" of the dedicatory verse); and perhaps young Abraham Cowley ("A.C." dedicatory verse). Thomas Tomkins, the musician-composer, dedicated four songs to Phineas in 1628. However, the most important literary friend of the decade was clearly Edward Benlowes. Twenty years Fletcher's junior, Benlowes became a friend and patron of Francis Quarles and of many other literary people at Cambridge in the early 1620s.

Langdale presents a fascinating sketch of Benlowes as a young "Maecenas of the North": a patron of arts and letters, a supporter of libraries and writers, and an author himself. Langdale notes that "Fletcher's poetry is rich in allusions to his friends, but the name of Benlowes appears everywhere with an impertinent prominence, even overshadowing that of the organist [Tomkins]. Both *The Purple Island* and *Sylva Poetica* were dedicated to him. Three copperplate engravings were bound in the first edition of the anatomical poem, bearing verse anagrams: 'Edward Benlowes, Sunwarde beloved'; 'Edovardus Benlowes, Durus, a Deo Benevolus'; while the third featured the arms of Fletcher . . . joined with those of Benlowes." Phineas; in dedicating to Benlowes his largest volume of published verse, writes: "For my self, I cannot account that worthy of your *Patronage*, which comes forth so short of my *Desires*. . . . In letting them abroad I desire to testifie, how much I preferre your desires before mine own, and how much I owe to *You* more then *any other*."

As Langdale also notes, "during the exact years when Fletcher was friendly with Benlowes, the presses of London and Cambridge commenced to publish his works, one after another, in a steady stream: *Locustae* and *The Apollyonists* in 1627; *Brittain's Ida* in 1628; *Sicelides* in 1631; *Joy in Tribulation* and *The Way to Blessedness* in 1632; and *The Purple Island, Piscatory Eclogs, Poeticall Miscellanies,* and *Sylva Poetica* in 1633. Was it a mere coincidence that the poet's desire to publish and his acquaintance with his admirer .were coetaneous?"[3] The answer is obviously negative; for although Benlowes surely provided a large boost to Fletcher's morale and undoubtedly subsidized much if not all costs of publication, it is doubtful that he increased Phineas' output very much or influenced his poetry. Despite the black moods of 1612 - 15, Phineas did not cease to view himself as a poet nor to be a producing poet. Indeed, most of his best poetry seems to have been written before he met Benlowes.

II *Mature Short Poems*

During the pre-Benlowes period, Phineas wrote a number of short mature poems that repay close reading and study. One, "To Mr. Jo. Tomkins," the distinguished musician, is a verse epistle in eight, nine-line stanzas *(abababccc),* dealing with Tomkins' move from King's College, Cambridge, to St. Paul's Cathedral, London, in 1619. It contrasts the lovely serene joys of country life with the dangers, vices, and intrigues of court life. The poem adopts the pastoral paraphernalia and mode appropriate to the men's old pastoral world, poetry and friends: "Thy strains to heare, / Old Chamus from his cell / Comes guarded with an hundred Nymphs around" (st. 2). The poem flatters Tomkins on his music and poetry, and presents Phineas' love and wish to be with him again in "countrey bowers" where they might forever sing and frame "sweet ditties" together. However, at the end of the poem, Phineas not only surrenders his old friend but, it seems, the whole pastoral world of his youth:

> Go little pipe; forever I must leave thee,
>
> . . .
>
> Go little pipe, for I must have a new:
> Farewell ye *Norfolk* maids, and Ida crue
> *Thirsil* will play no more; for ever now adeu.

Although its was a pastoral convention for the poet to hang up his pipes in times of sadness, the whole last stanza has an unmistakable ring of finality. In fact, neither "Thirsil"—the pastoral Phineas—nor, more significantly, the pastoral mode appears again in Phineas' writing.

Furthermore, this poem clearly suggests that Phineas not only has accepted his altered circumstance in life but intends to continue his writing:

> But seeing fate my happie wish refuses,
> Let me alone enjoy my low estate.
> Of all the gifts that fair *Parnassus* uses,
> Onely scorn'd povertie, and fortunes hate
> Common I finde to me, and to the Muses:
> But with the Muses welcome poorest fate.
>   Safe in my humble cottage will I rest;
>   And lifting up from my untainted breast
> A quiet spirit to heav'n securely live, and blest.

The style of the epistle, although pastoral in mode and conventions, is clearly simpler and tighter than his pastoral style of the preceding decade. One sees, for example, a more declarative construction, a simpler syntax, a cleaner prosody, and a less merely decorative verbalization.

III *Love Poems*

One way of discussing Phineas' miscellaneous short poems of maturity is by dividing them into meaningful subgroups, for Phineas wrote about equal numbers of short poems on love, morality, and religion. Another important category—wit poems—cuts across the others. Of these groups, the most impressive, surely, are the love poems, most of which appear to have been written within a few years of 1615. His "Epithalamium," a marvelous wedding celebration, was discovered in the manuscript with "Venus and Anchises" by Ethel Seaton. Little is known about the poem, about the bride and groom, or about why Fletcher excluded the poem from his published works; still, unmistakably by Phineas, it contains some of his very best poetry. A substantial poem of 244 lines in twenty stanzas, which vary from seven to thirty-six lines, its form is astonishingly irregular for Phineas Fletcher and very close to being free verse.

Lines 1 - 20 form an introduction which summons the "Fayre Norfolke maydes" and men to celebrate marriage with love and music: "Harke the woodes with Hymen ring / Hymen hilles and vallies sing." The second section (ll. 20 - 40) describes the Bridegroom's approach "Like glittering Hesperus"; a third section (ll. 40 - 50), "the Bride among the virgin traines"; section four (ll. 50 - 70), the wedding ceremony. Then, after "All rites are ended & a mutual kisse / Hath playd loves harbinger to future blisse," the fifth section (ll. 77 - 237) presents a long, detailed description of preparations for bed and consummation of the marriage. The consummation section ends, like Spenser's "Epithalamion," with the wish that it will prove fruitful and produce "A little nation" of children (237 - 44).

The long fifth section (77 - 237) is the most extraordinary part of the poem. Fletcher, using direct address to achieve great immediacy, even intimacy, describes a whole, very sensuous consummation scene that is presented as part of the war of the sexes and the game of love:

> Come o Come thow gentle swaine
> Now let loose the bitte and raygne
> To thy love soe kindlie heated
> Which soe oft she hath defeated
> Loose thy flame and iust desiring
> That long time with inward firing
> Vext thy heart thy hopes out-tyring
>
> She that with enchaunted smyling
> And sweet lookes thy soule beguiling
> She that with bewiching kisses
> Robd thy heart of former blisses
> And stole thy self out of thine eyes
> Now (happie now) there guiltie lies
> Guiltie of sweet theeveries
>
> Boldlie thow in Coverd Shade
> The daintie trembling theefe invade.

The light, sophisticated, semi-humorous, perhaps mock-heroic tone of the whole is nicely exemplified in the conclusion, which describes the long delayed consummation itself as an heroic victory:

> Now girt thy sweating browe wth Conquering bayes
> And tryumphs and victorious trophies raise
> Nor ever let that subiect province rest
> 'Till to thy hand she gratefull tribute payes,
> A litle nation, whose people blest
> Livelie beare portrayd in their lovelie faces
> A mixt proportion of each parentes graces.

Although the eroticism is handled with great delicacy, taste, and tact, most of the poem does concentrate upon erotic love. Since Spenser's "Epithalamion" (which also celebrates the physical and sensual aspects of love and ends with the wish for progeny) was probably known to Fletcher, it may have provided the general guideline of describing the wedding day itself as well as some other details beside the occasional refrain. However, the degree of erotic detail as well as the style, tone, and dominant impression of the poem are totally Fletcherian.

This very successful poem is full of excellent verses and various musical effects. To the traditional ingredients of wedding celebrations (flowers, songs, lovely young attendants, Hymen and related Classical figures, mirth, and joy), Fletcher has added a battle of the sexes and a celebration of erotic love that are as delicate and as sophisticated as those in *Venus and Anchises*, with which this poem has considerable affinity. Considered with the love poetry in *Sicelides* and with that which is still to be discussed, "Epithalamium" clearly indicates that Fletcher was a very good love poet who, without vulgarity or prudery, but with sensibility, taste, and delicacy, celebrated Eros in memorable poetry. This poem was probably excluded from his published works for the same reason that *Venus and Anchises* was: its eroticism was hardly appropriate for the rector of a country parish. Modern readers deserve to have this fine, unusual epithalamium, which is vintage Phineas Fletcher.[4]

Two other interesting and excellent poems, "Contemnenti" and "A Vow," are linked love poems:

Contemnenti

Continuall burning, yet no fire or fuel,
   Chill icie frosts in midst of summers frying,
A hell most pleasing, and a heav'n most cruel,
A death still living, and a life still dying,
     And whatsoever pains poore hearts can prove,
     I feel, and utter in one word, I LOVE.

Two fires, of love and grief, each upon either,
And both upon one poore heart ever feeding;
Chill cold despair, most cold, yet cooling neither,
In midst of fires his ycie frosts is breeding:
     So fires and frosts, to make a perfect hell,
     Meet in one breast, in one house friendly dwell.

> Tir'd in this toylsome way (my deep affection)
> I ever forward runne, and never ease me:
> I dare not swerve, her eye is my direction:
> A heavie grief, and weighty love oppresse me.
>> Desire and hope, two spurres, that forth compell'd me;
>> But awfull fear, a bridle, still withheld me.
>
> Twice have I plung'd, and flung, and strove to cast
> This double burden from my weary heart:
> Fast though I runne, and stop, they sit as fast:
> Her looks my bait, which she doth seld' impart.
>> Thus fainting, still some inne I wish and crave;
>> Either her maiden bosome, or my grave.

Such direct, personal lyricism is unusual for Phineas. The intensity and the sincerity of the suffering vitalize the otherwise conventional Petrarchan images which unify the poem: fire, ice, eyes, the disease of love, heaven and hell. The style could be described in one sense as rhetorical because of the high degree of parallelism, repetition, periodic construction, and rhetorical patterns of syntax. However, there is little of the excesses of adjectival coloration and verbal ornament of the pastoral Phineas. The poem not only rings true, but is truly an effective love complaint.

In "A Vow," a continuation of "Contemnenti," Phineas turns from the suffering, rejection, and unhappiness of a physical or mortal love experience to the higher love of God:

> Whither, poore soul, ah, whither wilt thou turn?
>> What Inne, what host (scorn'd wretch) wilt thou now chuse
>> The common host, and inne, death, grave, refuse thee.
> To thee great love, to thee I prostrate fall,
> That right'st in love the heart in false love swerved.

The image of the "inne" with which "Contemnenti" ends becomes the symbol of salvation in "A Vow." And the turn to God in the last stanza—"Thou never-erring Way, in thee direct me"—has the ring of conviction, substantial commitment, and an answer to the poet's depression and loss.

It is difficult not to see in these two poems a response to the events of 1612 - 15: the loss of love (Elizabeth Irby, it seems) and of hope (his Cambridge living, friends, and future), the depth and seriousness of despair, the turn to God involving a vow (holy orders). Together, the two poems form an impressive and very successful poetic whole. It is difficult to imagine that George Herbert had not read "A Vow" when he wrote his "Love" (II), which is so much like it, but which surely followed Fletcher's poem by several years.

IV   *Witty Love*

The anagramatic wit displayed by Phineas in "To my onely chosen Valentine and wife" reflects a changing literary taste around the court in the early seventeenth century for more verbal and poetic wit. At the center of this movement was probably John Donne, whose witty conceits, startling analogies, and verbal puns were at once intellectual and ingenious. Although Donne quickly became the "Monarch" of such wit, many others practiced it in diverse forms, including George Herbert and Phineas Fletcher. Herbert's "The Altar" and Fletcher's "Valentine" share an altar image and anagramatic ingenuity:

> *To my onely chosen Valentine and wife,*
> Ana-   MAYSTRESS ELISABETH VINCENT   -gram.
>   IS MY BRESTS CHASTE VALENTINE.

> Think not (fair love) that Chance my hand directed
>   To make my choice my chance; blinde Chance & hands
> Could never see what most my minde affected;
> But heav'n (that ever with chaste true love stands)
> Lent eyes to see what most my heart respected:
> Then do not thou resist what heav'n commands;
>   But yeeld thee his, who must be ever thine:
>   My heart thy altar is, my breast thy shrine;
> Thy name for ever is, *My Brests chaste Valentine.*

Today, scholars usually associate the witty seventeenth-century poem about love or about woman's inconstancy with Donne or with Cavalier poets like Suckling. However, Phineas composed at least three very fine examples; and one of these, "On womens lightnesse," begins,

Who sowes the sand? or ploughs the easie shore?
Or strives in nets to prison in the winde?
Yet I, (fond I) more fond, and senselesse more,

> Thought in sure love a womans thoughts to binde.
> Fonde, too fond thoughtes, that thought in love to tie
> One more inconstant then inconstancie! (St. 1)

The theme and the manner—especially the series of impossible
questions—are much like Donne's famous "Go and Catch a Falling
Star." Through five stanzas Phineas demonstrates and argues his
title-thesis with wit, pseudo-logical arguments, conceits, and diverse
analogies. He ends with a Donnean twist of direction, for even
sillier than trying to make a woman constant was loving her the way
she was—"but fondest I, / To grasp the winde, and love inconstan-
cie!"

The offended response of Lady Culpepper (or her daughter)
Phineas' friend from Kent, to "On womens lightnesse" produced
from Phineas another witty poem, "A reply upon the fair M.S.":

> A Daintie maid, that drawes her double name
> From bitter sweetnesse, (with sweet bitternesse)
> Did late my skill and faulty verses blame,
> And to her loving friend did plain confesse,
> That I my former credit foul did shame,
> And might no more a poets name professe:
>   The cause that with my verse she was offended,
>   For womens levitie I discommended.
>   (St. 1)

Phineas answers the charge that he was not a poet by agreeing; he
argues that poets "feigne, and make fine lies," whereas he told "the
truth, truth (ah)." He ingeniously develops this argument until,
with charm and barb, he applies the *coup de grace:*

> But give me leave to write as I have found:
> Like ruddy apples are their outsides bright,
> Whose skin is fair, the core or heart unsound;
> Whose cherry-cheek the eye doth much delight,
> But inward rottennesse the taste doth wound:
> Ah! were the taste so good as is the sight,
>   To pluck such apples (lost with self same price)
>   Would back restore us part of paradise.

He then performs a gallant reversal to compliment Lady
Culpepper:

> But if (fair-sweet) thy truth and constancie
>
> . . .
>
> If thy first love will first and last endure;
> Thou more then woman art, if time so proves thee,
> And he more then a man, that loved loves thee.

However, the polite, parlor-war-game of the sexes was not quite ended; Phineas apparently had to write "An Apologie for the premises to the Ladie Culpepper." With mock-gallantry, he repents and offers penance:

> But if so just excuse will not content ye,
> But still you blame the words of angry *Love;*
> Here I recant, and of those words repent me:
> In signe herof I offer now to prove,
>   That changing womens love is constant ever,
>   And men, though ever firm, are constant never.
>   (St. 5)

However, his even more witty and clever proof of the reverse proposition only demonstrates the original proposition. His conclusion, "All change; men for the worse, women for better," is a charming capitulation which can be interpreted favorably by either sex.

These three related poems are difficult to date, but they are not hard to admire as thoroughly delightful examples of the social game of love, the witty battle of the sexes that was played in the seventeenth century. That Phineas was able to produce such excellent examples clearly reveals still another dimension of his talent and literary sensibility. Nor were his wit-poems limited only to love and fickleness. The poem, "To Thomalin," is constructed around one extended metaphor or conceit: Phineas has "nothing" but his love left to give Tomkins. (Donne developed the same conceit in "Nocturnal upon St. Lucies.") The witty or analytic extension of a single dominating analogy, or conceit, has been considered the earmark of "metaphysical" poetry of the school of Donne. If so, one must conclude again that Phineas was very much in the forefront of changing literary tastes and directions in his age.

Like Donne, Herbert, and others, Phineas also uses wit in his serious poems. His poem "Upon the Contemplations of the B. [Bishop] of Excester, given to the Ladie E[lizabeth] W[illoughby] at

New-yeares-tide"—which seems to be preparing his patroness for death—may have preceded Donne's "Good Friday, 1613, Riding Westward":

> This little worlds two little starres are eyes;
> And he that all eyes framed, fram'd all others
> Downward to fall, but these to climbe the skies,
> There to acquaint them with their starrie brothers;
> Planets fixt in the head (their spheare of sense)
> Yet wandring still through heav'ns circumference,
> The Intellect being their Intelligence.
>   (St. 1)

Phineas' imagery drawn from astronomy and science, his syllogisms, his analytic reasoning, his paradox, and his broken speech-like rhythms are all features of the style of John Donne whose work he may have been reading in manuscript. At any event, the same style reappears in "These Asclepiads of Mr. H. S. translated and enlarged." Here, in expanding each of the four Latin lines into a stanza each of English verse, Phineas again reveals a style that is rhythmically tough and twisted, conceited, heavily analytic and image-laden, and that uses word play and paradox fully:

> [Sed Verbum fatuo sola Scientia]
> Thou Sunne of wisdome, knowledge infinite,
> Made folly to the wise, night to prophane;
> Be I thy Moon, o let thy sacred light
> Increase to th' full, and never, never wane:
> Wise folly set in me, fond wisdome rise,
> Make me renounce my wisdome, to be wise. (st. 3)

The important point is not whether Phineas, like other poets, knew and was influenced by Donne. Rather, it is that Phineas also belongs in the great "Monarchy of Wit" of which Thomas Carew considered Donne to be the Monarch. Phineas deserves a title at that court since he not only was writing this type of verse contemporaneously with Donne but also left behind more than a handful of very fine "wit" poems—poems both humorous and serious. This side of his talent should certainly be better known.

V   Moral-Religious Pieces

Another distinct subgroup of Phineas' short poems of maturity is the moral poetry written under the influence of Boethius' famous

Consolation of Philosophy, a work to which more than one poet has turned in times of stress or crisis. During the years around 1615, Phineas undoubtedly needed the consolation of philosophy; for, although it is impossible to date closely the eleven verse translations he made from Boethius' work, the sections he chose to translate are revealing: about half of these poems deal with the folly and the futility of pursuing worldly wealth and fame. He included two in his *Poeticall Miscellanies* (1633) and the rest in his last prose tract, *A Father's Testament* (1670). On the whole, theses poems appear to be very competent work and reflect the tightening style of his maturest verse. The themes closely correspond to those in his poems dating from 1615 - 25; they reveal a general, moral-religious concern as well as some very specific reading and study which the new priest was undertaking.

Perhaps the most characteristic poem of this period of Phineas' life and literature is "Against a rich man despising povertie." It is composed of five six-line stanzas *(ababcc),* the stanzaic form that Phineas seems to have preferred during these years. The rich man with whose estate Fletcher compares his own could be Sir Henry Willoughby, his patron:

> If well thou view'st us with no squinting eye,
> No partiall judgement, thou wilt quickly rate
> Thy wealth no richer then my povertie;
> My want no poorer then they rich estate:
>   Our ends and births alike; in this, as I;
> Poore thou wert born, and poore again shall die.

Fletcher indicates that he is content with his "little," but that the other man, with so much, wants even more. The poem, which has a definite Boethean moral-religious flavor, is a combination of "consolation" and conventional sermon piety. This mature poem, generally tight and solid, is competent but in no way extraordinary.

During the years after 1615, he was also translating and adapting "Certain of the royal Prophets Psalmes." The first one, Psalm 42, which he also set to "the tune of *Like the Hermite Poore,*" is consistent in theme with his works during the watershed period of life when, like the prophet, Phineas might well have felt,

> With grief I think on those sweet now past dayes,
> When to thy house my troopes with joy I led:
> We sang, we danc'd, we chanted sacred layes;
> No men so haste to wine, no bride to bed.
> Why droopst, my soul? why faint'st thou in my breast?

Something of his life is surely mirrored in the particular six Psalms which he chose to translate and include in the *Poeticall Miscellanies*. One of them, Psalm I, became the basis for what was probably his first prose work, *The Way to Blessedness, A Treatise or Commentary on the First Psalm*, which he dedicated to his patron, Sir Henry Willoughby, and which was published in 1633. Too long and too complex to paraphrase easily, this work presents a highly elaborate exegesis of the psalm with formal propositions, grounds, refutations, instructions, glosses, and about ten biblical allusions or quotations on every page. Since this work appears to have been written to impress someone with education and strong religious scruples about the author's religious credentials, it was written before 1621 to demonstrate to Willoughby that Phineas Fletcher was qualified and worthy of the rectorship at Hilgay.

The second prose tract, *Joy in Tribulation or a Consolation for Afflicted Spirits*, which appears to have been written between 1621 (the rectorship) and 1632 (the publication date) and, which attempts to prove that affliction is for man's own good, is a fascinating mixture of religious reasoning, scriptural example, aphorisms, and rhetorical metaphors and similes. This protracted "Consolation" was surely written for a country parish and for an unlearned audience; for its style, manner of development, and tone are notably simpler than those in *The Way to Blessedness*.

Just when he wrote his last prose work is uncertain. *A Father's Testament. Written long since for the benefit of the particular Relations of the Author . . . And now made Publick at the desire of Friends* was published posthumously in 1670. It presents general, religious-moral advice and Christian "instruction."

VI   *Late Religious Poems*

At the end of each of the twenty-one chapters of *A Father's Testament*, Phineas has affixed some verse: either his translations from Boethius or his own original poem. The ten original religious poems and the two hymns from the *Poeticall Miscellanie* comprise another subgroup of interest and value. Furthermore, they represent Fletcher's final poetical work.

The two hymns from *Poeticall Miscellanie* are devotional meditations. In the first, "An Hymne," Fletcher focuses attention upon the crucified Christ, by calling, stanza by stanza, upon his own soul, eyes, ears, and heart to "Wake" to Christ:

> Wake, O my soul; awake, and rise
> Up every part to sing his praise,
> Who from his spheare of glorie fell,
>   To raise thee up from death and hell:
> See how his soul, vext for thy sinne,
> Weeps bloud without, feels hell within:
>   See where he hangs;
>   heark how he cries:
>   Oh bitter pangs!
>   Now, now he dies.

The second "An Hymne" which is less ritualistic creates a very delicate, mellifluous, and quiet mood around the same object of devotion, Christ:

> Drop, drop, slow tears,
>   And bathe those beauteous feet,
> Which brought from heav'n
>   the news and Prince of peace:
> Cease not, wet eyes,
>   his mercies to intreat;
> To crie for vengeance
>   sinne doth never cease:
> In your deep flouds
>   drown all my faults and fears:
> Nor let his eye
>   see sinne, but through my tears.

Like these two hymns, the ten original poems in *A Father's Testament* reflect professional, mature work. However, as a whole, they lack any special excitement or emotional intensity. Some, like "The Beatific Vision," seem to be mere fragments exemplifying a subject in the prose work. Others tend to be somewhat talky and didactic, as if the rector of Hilgay were presenting appropriately liturgical subjects in verse for his flock: "The Vanity of Possessions," "The Search after God," "The Beatific Vision," "The Passage Perilous," "The Divine Lover," "The Divine Offer," "Israel's Yoke," "God's Image in Man," "The Light of Lights," "The Transfiguration of Man." Most of the poems make heavy use of rhetorical questions; and this technique produces a prayer-like effect of internal dialogue, sometimes with startling effect:

The Divine Lover

Me Lord? can'st thou mispend
one word, misplace one look on me?
   Call'st me thy Love, thy Friend?
   Can this poor soul the object be
Of these love-glances, those life-kindling eyes?
   Of all thy labour I the prize?
   Love never mocks, Truth never lies.
Oh how I quake: Hope fear, fear hope displaces:
I would, but cannot hope: such wondrous love amazes.

Ultimately, these poems convey more a sense of divine duty than divine drama; more a sense of the conscious application of Fletcher's poetic talent to the clergyman's office than of an inner struggle of faith being transformed into poetry. They convey the digested truths of the Church in an official voice. As with much of his earliest verse, these poems tend to be poetic formulas and clichés bound up into respectable poems. They are, however, much surer and better than the early ones. If they are indeed his final poetry, as they appear to be (1635 - 50), they form also a quiet and peaceful end to a long, diverse, and prolific poetic career. They speak with a respectable, firm, and dignified voice in the service of church and God and poetry.

CHAPTER 9

Giles and Phineas Through the Centuries

I Seventeenth Century

TO measure the significance or impact of a writer, whether major or minor, upon the literature of his own nation and language or its readers is highly desirable but is, of course, exceptionally difficult. This task is particularly so when it involves not only a much earlier period but also by modern standards a general paucity of records and information. However, the available evidence indicates that the Fletchers, particularly Phineas, represented a distinct literary force in their age. What Cory, about half a century ago called "The School of the Fletchers" may be less flamboyantly visible today than its contemporary "Tribe of Ben," but it is far more tangible than, for example, the "School of Donne."[1]

The center and origin of the Fletcher group was clearly Cambridge University. The original "coterie" about which Phineas was so self-conscious in his writings from 1605 - 15 included himself and Giles; the two musician-poets, John and Thomas Tomkins; Samuel Woodford; and perhaps his father Giles, Sr., who figures conspicuously in Phineas' consciousness during those years. Later, others were involved: Francis Quarles, who became one of the most popular literary figures of the day; Edward Benlowes (whose poem *Theophila*, according to Douglas Bush, "represents metaphysical religious poetry in *excelsis* and *in extremis*"); Izaak Walton; perhaps Abraham Cowley; and others.

But there is a larger, more important sense in which a "School of the Fletchers" has impressed itself upon critics and scholars. Cory, for example, writes that the influence of the Fletchers was far greater than has generally been realized. They founded a distinct school of poetry which outlived the chilling influence of the Restoration. Even in the eighteenth century the school survived in the work of William Thompson, one of the earliest romanticists of that period. In Milton's day, most of the Cantabrigians, Crashaw, Joseph Beaumont, Thomas Robinson, and others wrote more or less in their manner. In his boyhood Milton was enlisted in the School of the Fletchers and their influence is traceable even in his mature poems. Any study of Spenserian material in Milton, then, should include an elaborate examination of the work of the School of the Fletchers.[2]

The extent of the direct influence of the Fletchers on particular writers is, however, difficult to gauge. Some, like Thompson, declared their indebtedness; for others, like Milton, there exists a history of commentary and evidence from readers and critics on the "influence" and "borrowings"; but others, like Owen Feltham, whose *Resolves* (1628) opens with reference to *The Purple Island*, seen merely to reflect awareness of some Fletcher work.[3]

Another form of evidence of the Fletchers' reputation in their own era appears in that rapidly emerging new genre of the last half of the seventeenth century—the short biography or collection of the lives of "Worthies." The Fletchers are included in the most famous collection of the age, Thomas Fuller's *The History of the Worthies of England* (1662), as well as in William Winstanley's *The Lives of the most Famous English Poets* (1687), the first biography of English literary "greats." In fact, Winstanley devotes more space to Phineas Fletcher than to John Milton, George Herbert, and many another of the age's now more famous writers. He writes of Phineas: "This learned person, Son and Brother to two ingenious Poets, himself the third, not second to either . . . in Poetical fame exceeded his two Brothers, in that never enough to be celebrated Poem, entitled *The Purple Island.*" Winstanley also speaks of Phineas as "that Divine Poet and Philosopher," and Izaak Walton, as previously noted, the single most famous biographer of the century, complimented Phineas highly. In 1633, Francis Quarles described Phineas as "The Spencer of this age."[4]

In evaluating these bits and pieces about the Fletchers, one must remember that Spenser, Shakespeare, Ben Jonson, John Milton and many another now famous writer received considerably less biographical attention than Phineas Fletcher. In short, the evidence from the seventeenth century indicates clearly that Phineas Fletcher was a known and influential literary figure in the first half of the century (better known personally than Giles, Jr.) and that the brothers affected a number of other writers of the age, especially those who were connected with Cambridge and the Fletchers' literary coterie in the first third of the century.

II *Eighteenth Century*

The Restoration and Augustan age mark a sharp decline, even eclipse, in the Fletchers' fame and impact. In fact, except for William Thompson and an occasional note, these writers seem to disappear for almost a century (*ca.* 1670 - 1770). The same fate befell most of the poets of their age, especially the Metaphysical and religious poets. Neoclassical canons of taste and rules, as spelled out by Dryden, Addison, and Pope, found little of worth in the "Former age." Late in the century, however, a change of literary taste and sensibility occurred (pre-Romantic) which involved the reviving of the "antiquities" which had been ignored or denigrated by the neoclassical age. Thomas Percy's *Reliques of Ancient English Poetry* (1765) marks the beginning of a wave that brought the Fletchers to a new and larger audience. In 1771, when Phineas' *Piscatory Eclogues, with other Poetical Miscellanies* was published in Edinburgh, it was the first edition of his poetry in almost 150 years (since 1633); and it was "illustrated with notes critical and explanatory." In 1783 in London was published *The Purple Island or the Isle of Man, an Allegorical poem by Phineas Fletcher, esteemed the Spenser of his Age to which is added Christ's Victorie and Triumph, A poem in four parts by Giles Fletcher.*

The first revival of critical attention for the Fletcher brothers was begun by Headley, for he included both poems and a biographical sketch of Phineas and Giles in his *Selected Beauties of Ancient English Poetry*, (London, 1787). He followed this edition with a "Supplement" in which his critical attention to Phineas became more detailed and extensive. The flavor of Headley's very affirmative evaluation of Phineas is nicely captured in his concluding sentence: "It is to his honour that Milton read and imitated him, as every attentive reader of both poets must soon discover. He is eminently entitled to a very high rank among our old English classics."

III *Nineteenth Century*

Thereafter, and throughout the nineteenth century, the Fletchers' poetry appears with notable regularity in anthologies, collections, and various editions, both with and without commentary or critical—biographical notes. One small indication of the almost complete reversal of literary fate that the Fletchers underwent from the eighteenth to the nineteenth century is Alexander Chalmers' massive and monumental *Works of the English Poets* (1810; 21 volumes). Samuel Johnson's *Lives of the English Poets*, the epitome of eighteenth-century criticism, which Chalmers used as the foundation of his work, made no mention of the Fletchers or their poetry. Chalmers, however, added substantial "lives" of Giles and Phineas as well as 126 pages of their poetry (including all of *Christ's Victorie and Triumph*, *The Purple Island*, *Piscatorie Eclogues*, *Elisa*, and parts of *Poeticall Miscellanie*). In short, a substantial distribution and revival of the poetry of Giles, Jr. and Phineas Fletcher occurred throughout the nineteenth century. Along with this renewal of interest developed an interesting body of criticism.

One notices several tendencies in nineteenth-century criticism before Grosart, whose elaborate and often hyperbolic criticism marks a special high point in the Fletcher literary impact. The value judgments of critics, as usual, vary widely; however, the Fletchers are clearly more praised than condemned; they are also universally afforded a place among "the poets," even by hostile critics. Most critics and editors, perhaps following Headley and before him Benlowes, emphasize their place in a literary dynasty. Cattermole, for example, writes that "The family of Fletcher was rendered illustrious in the literary history of the Seventeenth Century by a constellation of poetic power"; or, as Robert Southey puts it: "No single family has ever, in one generation produced three such poets as Giles and Phineas Fletcher, and their cousin the dramatist."[5]

The negative response to Phineas dwells mostly on *The Purple Island*, a work almost universally condemned. However, as the critics move to general evaluation of the poet, a markedly upward evaluation occurs; and the view of R. Anderson is exemplary:

but not withstanding these gross deficiencies of judgment, and the infelicity of subjects, he has a great deal of genuine fire, is frequently happy in similes, admirable in epithets and compound words, and superior to almost all his contemporaries in the unstudied flow of his versification. . . . it is but doing justice to the effusions of a real poetical mind, to acknowledge that however thwarted by untowardness of subject, or corrupted by false taste, the compositions of Phineas Fletcher entitle him to a high rank among our old English classics.[6]

Jerrold points to the many passages in *The Purple Island* "of singular beauty" and advises wise readers not to overlook them. Jerrold also reflects the tendency to praise Phineas' prosody: "in his imagery he frequently distinguishes himself by his boldness and originality; in his use of 'conceits' he is no less happy than other poets of his century who made of conceit-poetry something of a new power; and of his epigrammatic condensation many instances may be cited." Chalmers concludes, like most other critics in the century, by repeating Headley's conclusion: "He is eminently entitled to a very high rank among our old English classics."[7]

Giles is somewhat less attended but is more highly and more consistently praised than Phineas. Anderson is again characteristic: "The poetry of Giles Fletcher is characterized by sublimity, animation, and splendor, with an unfortunate intermixture of extravagance; it has many beauties and many conceits; but, after making every deduction which criticism requires, his *Christ's Victory and Triumph* is a performance of which both poetry and religion may justly boast . . . [He] has never yet received the honours he deserves" (p. 490).

Among critics who often treat the brothers together, a pattern of responses can be discerned. After specific criticisms, the Fletchers' impact upon their own age is noted, the unwarranted lack of attention afforded by the eighteenth century is lamented, and a usually affirmative judgment is passed. Southey, for example, observed that "The two Fletchers are the best poets of the school of Spenser. . . . Deservedly eminent as they were in their own age, neither Browne nor the Fletchers are noticed in Cibber's *Lives of the Poets*" (p. 749). Willmott notes that "Giles Fletcher, the author of one of the finest religious poems to which the early part of the seventeenth century gave birth, has not received the attention due to his genius, either from his contemporaries, or from posterity. Yet in him and his brother Phineas we behold the two most gifted followers of Spenser."[8] Chalmers concludes that the Fletchers "remain in possession of a degree of invention, imagination, spirit, and sublimity, which we seldom meet with among poets of the seventeenth century before we arrive at Milton" (p. 54).

Grosart's criticism appears in the long "Memorial-Introduction" of his editions of the complete poems of Phineas (1869) and of Giles (1876). Although Grosart's views are too long and multifaceted to summarize, he clearly presented the most superlative and the least balanced Fletcher criticism. Grosart points out admirable qualities, presents valuable information, but most of the justifiable praise which he heaps on both poets, seems unacceptable because of his extreme bias and defensiveness. However, despite obvious defects, Grosart's work about the Fletchers should be neither discounted nor overlooked. Furthermore, Grosart exemplifies a distinct fact about Phineas Fletcher: his work has produced over the centuries a group of recognizable devotées such as Benlowes, Quarles, Headley, Grosart, Boas, and Langdale.

IV   Twentieth Century

The twentieth-century response to Giles, Jr. and Phineas has been far more mixed than that of the nineteenth. Grosart's work apparently stimulated renewed scholarly and editorial interest. In 1903, Orinda Booklets put out a small edition, *Phineas Fletcher: Selected Poetry;* in 1905, *The Spenser of his Age* (selected poetry) was issued by J. R. Rutlin Company; in 1909, F. S. Boas edited for Cambridge University Press the standard two-volume *Poetical Works of Giles and Phineas Fletcher.* In 1927 Ethel Seaton published her discovery of the Sion College manuscript of several of Phineas' poems, *Venus and Anchises, and other Poems.* In 1937, A. B. Langdale's *Phineas Fletcher: Man of Letters, Science and Divinity* appeared; it is the most thorough piece of scholarship on either poet to date. There have also been in this century some thirty to forty scholarly articles, notes, or doctoral dissertations on either one or both poets. Most anthologies continue to include some selection of their work, and historical studies of the period seldom fail to mention them. Although the amount of scholarship on them has increased in this century, the volume has not been impressive when compared to that about some of their contemporaries; and one reason for this has again been literary fashions and tastes. The dominant taste in the early part of this century, stimulated by Ezra Pound, T. S. Eliot, F. R. Leavis, M. Murray, and other critics, for Metaphysical verse in the Donne tradition has clearly worked against the Fletchers. The fashionable movement for many years was away from the poetry of Milton, of Spenser, and of their kindred spirits like the Fletchers.

Twentieth-century scholars, critics, and teachers, preoccupied with different literary traditions and emphases, have been contented to think of the Fletchers in literary historical clichés; and the most common ones are "imitators of Spenser," "of the school of

Spenser,'' or as the minor bridge between two major poets—Spenser and Milton. Modern anthologies in the last thirty years or so have tended to represent them with select passages from a single long work by each (for Phineas, the selection is inevitably and unfortunately from *The Purple Island*). The type of critical-scholarly comments made about them strongly supports what the anthology selections suggest: they are being read neither representatively nor carefully.

Among those scholars who have read the Fletchers and responded to them, the criticism is clearly mixed. A variety of distinct voices can be heard. H. E. Cory, who views them as a separable "school" of poetry is also troubled and disaffected by their work: "queer stuff," "freakish poems," "strange perverted works." He describes them as "these curious, half-diseased, half-divine poets." Not even Cory, however, is quite so negative as D. C. Shelden is about Giles:

Even the most casual reader of Giles Fletcher's poetry can hardly fail to be impressed by its obviously derivative character. Almost every page of his work reveals what seem to be the most flagrant appropriations of material from his predecessors. The classics, medieval literature, and the Elizabethan poets have apparently been ransacked to provide his poetic embellishments, and the over-mastering influence of Spenser appears in nearly every line. Mythological allusions, often irrelevant, often tasteless, are required for the simplest natural events. The concrete force of the Gospel narrative which forms the basis of Fletcher's principal poem is softened and obscured by elaborate allegories, all of them second-hand. Even the minutiae of diction and versification represent borrowings from earlier poets.[9]

R. G. Baldwin sees like qualities in Phineas, but he arrives at rather different conclusions:

The conservativism that characterizes very nearly everything Fletcher wrote is not so much the reflection of an unoriginal cast of mind as the inevitable concomitant of a whole-hearted dedication to truth and good form. In his poetry this led to his seeking the correct, effective, agreed manner of expressing a given experience. In his thinking, it led him to search out the fixed and established, the traditonal and familiar, from one point of view the commonplace. For our times he is therefore a valuable source of renaissance ideas in their clearest, most settled, simplest form.[10]

Most twentieth-century critics have not shared the views of Shelden and, in different terms, those of Baldwin. M. M. Mahood, for

example, notes: "these brothers deserve to be regarded as the dis-
seminators of a new poetic manner, rather than as the last ex-
ponents of an effete style" (p. 171). A. M. Witherspoon and F. J.
Warnke are not alone in speaking of "their strange colors." In fact,
this was the very area in which Courthope found their major
defects"—"the passion for novelty . . . in the manner of expressing
conceptions."[11]

Langdale is almost unique in finding "the most original feature
of Phineas Fletcher's life and writings . . . [to be] his scientific in-
terests" in *The Purple Island*. Although Langdale's is not a critical
study of the poetry, he felt Phineas' main faults to be his conceits,
his artificialities of grammar and vocabulary, and the structural
faults in his main works. On the affirmative side, he notes,

Despite its weaknesses, there are many reasons why Fletcher's poetry has
been and will be read. There are recurring trills of music in its measures
and flashes of color in its similes. When the poet hammers out lines in
righteous anger, his phrases become forceful, never spiteful, but strong and
true as steel. There is a manly vigor about all these poems which has been
overlooked and which should recommend *The Apollyonist*, particularly, to
more readers.

The most recent, lengthy and good, published critical study is
Joan Grundy's *The Spenserian Poets* (1969) in which one might
reasonably expect the Spenserian and other derivative qualities of
the Fletchers to be stressed. Since quite the opposite treatment occurs, Grundy's conclusions are well worth noting: "No snap judgment on the Fletchers is therefore possible. They are both, but especially Phineas, more complicated than at first appears. And the
complexities of their moral make-up are repeated in their literary
make-up. In the models they choose to follow, they are quite
bewilderingly eclectic." She also notes that "neither 'baroque' nor
'Spenserian' used separately is sufficient to describe the Fletchers."
She concluded that "both are better poets than has yet been
acknowledged."[12]

In summarizing the Fletchers' impact "through the centuries,"
one can quarrel very little with Courthope's observation that "their
artistic merits have been variously judged" (p. 133).

V *Critical Questions*

Both historically and critically, appreciation and interest in the
Fletchers has been decidedly mercurial. More than that of most

writers, their impact has followed the shifting winds of taste and
fashion; nonetheless the responses to the Fletchers through the centuries also indicate certain recurrent critical questions which have
weighed heavily in the critical estimates. These involve principally
their "Spenserianism," their place and significance in literary
history, and their relationship to each other.

The relationship of the Fletchers' poetry to Spenser has been the
single most noted and discussed aspect of their work. It has been
the basis for labelling them followers of Spenser or of the "school"
of Spenser; for indicating not only Spenser's great influence but the
Fletchers' lack of originality; it has been used as evidence of their
lackeying and their plagiarism. Langdale devoted a whole chapter,
"The Master and the Apprentice," to "Phineas Fletcher's
dependence upon Spenser." He concluded that "Spenser's influence upon his follower was even greater than previous students
have indicated"; however, he also added that "Grosart was foolish
to allow himself to be stung by the catcalls of plagiarism, because,
whatever may be the relation of Fletcher and Spenser, it is not
plagiaristic" (p. 131).

Spenser's influence upon them is apparent; *its extent has been
grossly exaggerated.* Unfortunately, it has more often than not
diverted attention from genuine critical evaluation, has been used
as a convenient "epitaph" by critics whose tastes ran in other directions, and has provided an easily remembered category for literary
historians. Some points relative to these evaluations should be
clarified. Both Giles, Jr., and Phineas paid homage in their work to
Spenser, along with others who influenced them, including Du Bartas, Vergil, and Sanazaro. Of Phineas' four statements of homage to
Spenser, three occur in *The Purple Island*, which is also his most
Spenserian poem. Historically, those who have used the label
"Spenserian" most have been also the most critical of the Fletchers'
poetry; and the epithet clearly obfuscates the originality that the
Fletchers do possess. Most who read the Fletchers' poetry objective-
ly and in depth will surely agree at least with Grundy that the term
"Spenserian" is insufficient to describe either or both of the
Fletchers; furthermore, the influence of Vergil and Du Bartas
appears to have been even stronger than Spenser's—and, has yet to
be explored fully.

In terms of literary history, the term "Spenserian" has also been
used to weave the Fletchers neatly into the literary fabric of the first
half of the seventeenth century. It has proved especially useful with
that old clichéd design which divides seventeenth-century poetry

into the "schools" of Spenser, Donne, and Jonson. Although "Spenserian" has been the dominant twentiety-century classification of them, it has not been the only one. Many critics see them as the "bridge" or the "link" between two great poets. Considering the multiple relationships of the Fletchers to Spenser and Milton, this view has considerable justification and merit. Also, Courthope has not been the only one to stress their "wit" and its significance. Witherspoon and Warnke note in *Seventeenth Century Poetry and Prose*, that " 'Wit' unites the varied poets of seventeenth-century England, for it underlies equally the striking antitheses and surprising epithets of the brothers Giles and Phineas Fletcher, the pithy epigrams and epitaphs of Jonson, and the paradoxes, puns, and conceits of Donne and Herbert" (p. 709). They then relate such wit to a sense of irony and to "a whole mode of vision" of the era. They also stress how much the Fletchers learned "from the continental poets who had formed the highly colored, overwrought variety of High Baroque poetry—a poetic manner ultimately very different from Spenser's serene and controlled Renaissance style" (p. 708).

Most studies treat the Fletcher brothers as essentially synonymous, as basically interchangeable. A good deal of the commentary or criticism assumes an attitude much like the following: "The relationship between Giles and Phineas Fletcher in their work as well as in their lives, is a close one: they are brother poets as well as brothers. The area of agreement between them, in matters of taste, belief, and style, is very great, and the resemblance of each to the other is stronger than the resemblance of either to any other writer."[13] As the Fletchers' statements in both *Christ's Victorie and Triumph* and *The Purple Island* show, they were working together very closely and self-consciously so for at least five years; and they borrowed bits from each other and read the same authors, Du Bartas, Sanazaro, Vida, and Spenser. As Christian sacred singers, *vates*, and mythologists who were burning with a grand Christian vision of cosmic unity and who were producing English epic poetry in the new Baroque fashion, the Fletchers are most alike; and in this respect they are also most original, most influential—with Milton especially—and most important in English literary history. However, although this summary fairly well characterizes Giles' writing career, it characterizes only one segment of Phineas' work.

There are, in fact, many notable differences between them. To begin with, the brothers' poetic careers were actually quite different. Giles wrote and published his few short poems and epyllion within one decade, 1600 - 1610; whereupon, his poetic career apparently ended. Phineas' career began about the same time as Giles', but it continued throughout most of his life, spanned some forty or fifty years of writing, and was notably long, prolific, and many-sided. Phineas' career reveals patterns and aspects completely lacking in Giles': the Vergillian pattern; the distinct pastoral period and involvement; the literary coterie; the autobiographical dimension of his work; the sizable body of amorous, erotic literature; his many Muses (Chamus, Venus, Urania, Love, Science, God).

This diversity stands in sharp contrast to the singularity of Giles' "sacred Muse." Also, Giles appears serious, intensely dedicated, introverted, inspired but humorless, and a slow, careful worker. Phineas seems enthusiastic, mercurial (even childlike at times), exuberantly prolific but short on critical judgment, a man of diverse mood, essentially outgoing and indefatigable.

In short, they are very different kinds of poets and personalities who for perhaps five years collaborated closely and shared ideas in an important and productive way, as did Wordsworth and Coleridge very much later. The evidence suggests, in fact, that after 1610 they had nothing further to do with each other poetically. At that point, their careers as writers sharply diverged. Giles' career ended; Phineas went off in a number of very different directions during the next forty years.

Many intrinsic values also exist in the poetry that each Fletcher brother left behind for future readers. Giles' body of poetry, much smaller and more consistent in quality, is easier to appreciate, and in general, it has been so appreciated in this century. But Phineas' poetry, which is more impressive overall than Giles', has certainly been neither properly examined nor evaluated by the twentieth century—nor, in truth, by any age, including his own—for two very clear, very precise reasons.

The first reason is Phineas' *The Purple Island*. A Study of the response to Phineas Fletcher, poet, reveals through the centuries that *The Purple Island* is unmistakably an albatross around his poetic neck. Since the late seventeenth century that work has been virtually synonymous with his name. For example, it has served as the basis for almost every piece of criticism; and too often it is the only work either mentioned or apparently read. As already noted, it is almost universally disliked—even by critics who finally praise more than denounce the poet. Furthermore, it forms the basis for his supposed lifelong "Spenserianism." Certainly he is responsible for its publication and so must bear its weight. However, even after justly denigrating his critical faculties and judgment, one must admit that a grotesque historical injustice as well as misrepresentation has occurred.

The second reason must also have been partly Phineas' fault because a number of his best works were either not published, were published anonymously so as to be unrelated to the rector, or are out of print. *Sicelides, Venus and Anchises,* "Epithalamium," and the late lyrics from *A Fathers Testament* have been clearly identified as his only in the twentieth century; and no edition contains all of his poetical work. Unfortunately, the seven poems in the Sion College manuscript can only be read in Ethel Seaton's little-known edition of them that is now out of print—as are Phineas' three books of religious prose.[14]

In short, the complete canon of Phineas' work has been little known—and even less considered in evaluating him. This situation is regrettable, especially since the body of poetry that Phineas did publish in his lifetime is larger than that of Donne, Herbert, Jonson, Sidney, or any cavalier poet. In size, it not only rivals the work of Spenser and Milton but also reveals the great variety of a major author: epic, drama, pastoral eclogues, epithalamia and hymens, elegies, long and short narratives (romantic, theological, nationalistic, and amorous), a sizable and diverse body of occasional verse, psalms, hymns, translations, devotional pieces, secular love and erotic songs, and so forth. Also, the meters of both Giles and Phineas were, as Courthope noted, "peculiar to themselves." Langdale counted thirty-six varieties in Phineas' poetry alone.

Modern readers may well find that their personal preferences concerning Phineas' work differ from those of past critics. They may join me in finding him best as an amorous and erotic poet, as a court wit, and as a short narrative and dramatic poet—and least impressive as the self-conscious *vates* of Christian heroic poetry. *The Purple Island* is an unmistakable disaster—both in its own right and, especially, in its relationship to his reputation. Removing that dragon from the cave entrance, however, reveals some extraordinary hidden treasure.

Phineas Fletcher wrote some other bad poems, but many more that are uncommonly good. He is one of those poets of great extremes; and he is also one who began somewhat late and matured slowly. His career is long and marked by changes of direction and style. It is too diverse, too multifaceted, too radically uneven to allow easy classification or simple evaluation. To read him fully and carefully—especially in conjunction with Giles, Jr.—is, at the very least, a pleasantly surprising experience; for Phineas and Giles Fletcher, Jr. were poets indeed—as well as members of an astonishing talented literary family.

Notes and References

Chapter One

1. Rev. R. Cattermole and Rev. H. Stebbing, eds., *The Sacred Classics*, (London, 1834), XXI, 69.

2. A. B. Langdale, *Phineas Fletcher, Man of Letters, Science and Divinity* (New York: 1937) contains the most complete, detailed genealogy and family history; unless otherwise noted, all biographical information comes from Langdale or one of the following biographical sources: Thomas Fuller, *History of the Worthies of England [1661]*, ed. P. A. Nutall, 3 vols. (London, 1840); Alexander Chalmers, *The General Biographical Dictionary* (London, 1812 - 17); *Dictionary of National Biography*, ed. L. Stephen and S. Lee (London, 1885 - 1900; and "Supplements"); A. B. Grosart, "Memoir" and "Notes," *The Poems of Phineas Fletcher* (Fuller Worthies Library, 1869), vol. I and "Memorial Introduction" and "Notes," *The Complete Poems of Giles Fletcher* (London, (1876); D. C. Shelden, "Introduction" and "Notes", "The Complete Poems of Giles Fletcher, the Younger" (Doct. Diss. University of Wisconsin, 1938); William Winstanley, *Lives of the most famous English Poets* (London, 1687).

Chapter Two

1. Biographical information about Giles Fletcher is particularly scarce. This sketch represents a synthesis of material from Langdale, Grosart, Boas, Shelden, and the *Dictionary of National Biography*. Shelden includes a copy of the whole Fuller biography; quotations throughout are from that copy. The birth date which was established by Langdale (p. 12) is almost certainly correct. Giles' birth in London was not recorded at the Cranbrook rectory unlike that of other members of the family.

2. Additional biographical-literary information comes from the Fletcher brothers' poetry, particularly Phineas': cf., e.g., *Christ's Victorie and Triumph*, IV, 49 - 50, and prefatory verse to it by Phineas on their joint literary activities. On the coterie, see H. E. Cory, "Spenser, The School of the Fletchers, and Milton," *University of California Publications in Modern Philology*, II, 5 (1912), 311 - 73.

3. On Milton's debt see Cory, *loc. cit.*; J. H. Handford, *A Milton Handbook* (New York, 1946), pp. 135 - 42, 263 - 64; G. McColley, *Paradise Lost* (Chicago, 1940), pp. 118 - 25, 166 - 68; E. C. Baldwin, "Milton and

Phineas Fletcher," *Journal of English and Germanic Philology*, XXXIII (1934), 544 - 46.

4. All quotations used throughout this study from the works of Giles and Phineas Fletcher, unless otherwise indicated, come from F. S. Boas, ed., *The Poetical Works of Giles and Phineas Fletcher*, 2 vols. (Cambridge, England, 1908). Above, Boas, I, pp. 7 - 8. Shelden, pp. 5 - 7, presents details and documentation on the Fellowship and Nevile, who may have been related to Phineas through the Yorkshire Fletcher-Neviles.

5. Spedding, *Bacon's Life and Letters*, VI, p. 172, quoted by Langdale, p. 78.

6. Giles Fletcher, *The Reward of the Faithful*, by A. B. for B. Fisher (n.p., 1623); the eleven pages in the "Epistle Dedicatory" are not numbered; all quotations from the British Museum copy.

7. Quoted in full by Grosart, "Memorial-Introduction," pp. 10 - 12.

8. Boas, I, pp. 14, prefatory verse to *Christ's Victorie and Triumph*.

9. Boas, I, pp. 1 - 3; printed by permission of Cambridge University Press. My stanzaic numbering.

10. Boas, I, pp. vii, 266 - 268; again by permission. My stanzaic numbering.

11. Donne and Crashaw quotations from *Seventeenth Century Verse and Prose*, Volume One: 1600 - 1660, eds. H. C. White, R. C. Wallerstein, R. Quintana (New York, 1951), pp. 78, 386.

12. On the application of these terms in literary study, see Wylie Sypher, *Four Stages of Renaissance Style: Transformations in Art and Literature, 1400 - 1700* (Garden City, N.Y., 1955); Frank J. Warnke, *European Metaphysical Poetry* (New Haven, 1961), pp. 20ff as applied to Giles; Roy Daniells, *Milton, Mannerist and Baroque* (Toronto, 1963); L. Nelson, *Baroque Lyric Poetry* (New Haven 1961).

Chapter Three

1. I. G. [*sic*] *A Refutation of Apology for Actors* (London, 1615) in Lily B. Cambell, *Divine Poetry and Drama in Sixteenth Century England* (Berkeley and Los Angeles, 1959), p. 5.

2. Boas, I, pp. 10 - 13.

3. Merritt Y. Hughes, *John Milton; Complete Poems and Major Prose* (New York, 1957), pp. 669 - 70; all Milton quotations are from this text.

4. As indication of popular beliefs leading to this kind of separation of roles for both poet and poetry, Peter Martyr Vermigli, *Common Places* (London, 1583), Pt. 3, Cap. 12, states: "betweene Poems divine and humane, this is the difference: that humane Poems doe set foorth the renoune of kings, princes, feelds, cities, regions, castels, women, marriages, and sometime of brute beast. But divine Poems doe onlie sing of God, and celebrate him onlie."

5. See Watson Kirkconnell, *The Celestial Cycle* (Toronto, 1952); or J. M. Evans, *Milton and the Genesis Tradition* (Oxford, 1968).

6. Du Bartas, *La Muse Chrestienne* (1574) laid the foundation for the tradition. His influence in England, as well as the background relative to some of the writers Giles mentions, is well described by Lily B. Cambell, (note 1), pp. 1 - 5 *et passim*. See also James P. Bobrick, "Giles Fletcher and the Hexameral Tradition," (Doct. diss., Boston University, 1973), a tradition in which Du Bartas is also important.

7. Hughes, pp. 728 - 29.

Chapter Four

1. My review is indebted particularly to F. J. Warnke, *European Metaphysical Poetry*, pp. 20ff *et passim;* and Shelden's and Grosart's introductions.

2. On the relationship of Giles and Spenser, much has been written: see Joan Grundy, *The Spenserian Poets* (London, 1969); Cory, "Spenser, The School of the Fletchers, and Milton" (note 2, Ch. 2); Shelden, pp. 68ff. Arno Esch, *Giles Fletcher's 'Christ's Victorie and Triumph': Eine Studie zum Epenstil des englishen Barock* (n.p., 1937); J. D. Wilson, "Giles Fletcher and the Faerie Queene," *Modern Language Review*, V (1910), 493 - 94; Jerome S. Dees, "The narrator's Voice in *The Faerie Queene, Christ's Victorie and Triumph*, and *The Locusts or Apolyonists*," (Doct. diss. University of Illinois, 1968).

3. The quotations are from *Renaissance England*, eds. R. Lamson and H. Smith (New York, 1942), p. 209. This Fletcher stanza is a composite of III, 4 - 5.

4. On Baroque features in Giles poetry, see especially M. M. Mahood, *Poetry and Humanism* (Oxford, 1950; rpt, New York, 1967), pp. 171 - 75; and Grundy, "Giles and Phineas Fletcher," *The Spenserian Poets* (London, 1969), pp. 181 - 204.

5. Quotations from Donne, Herbert, Crashaw are from *Seventeenth Century Verse & Prose* (note 11, Ch. 2).

6. See note 3, Ch. 2.

7. MacDonald, pp. 152 - 53; *The Works of the British Poets, with Lives of the Authors*, ed. Ezekiel Sanford (Philadelphia, 1819), V, p. 92; *Selected Works of the British Poets (Chaucer to Jonson)*. (London, 1831), p. 807; *The Sacred Classics*, eds. R. Cattermole and H. Stebbing (London, 1835), Vol. XXI, p. 83.

8. Douglas Bush, *Mythology and the Renaissance Tradition in English Poetry* (1932; rpt. New York, 1963), p. 166.

9. The Warnke quotation is from *Seventeenth-Century Prose and Poetry*, ed. A. M. Witherspoon and F. J. Warnke, 2nd. ed. (New York, 1963), p. 709; see their discussion of Baroque. See also Faye P. Whitaker,

"Giles Fletcher's *Christ's Victorie and Triumph:* A Study of Some Developing Strains of Seventeenth Century Religious Poetry," (Doct. diss., Northwestern University, 1974).

10. Shelden, pp. 111 - 12; *A Complete Edition of the Poets of Great Britain,* ed. R. Anderson (Edinburgh, 1793), IV, pp. 485 f.

Chapter Five

1. *Christ's Victorie and Triumph,* IV, 49, Giles describing Phineas; for the general biography, see note 2, Ch. 1; Langdale and Grosart form the foundation on Phineas here and hereafter.

2. *The Poetical Works of Edmund Spenser,* eds. J. C. Smith and E. De Selincourt (Oxford, 1912), p. 418.

3. Langdale, Chs. IV and V, contain excellent discussion of these important matters.

4. Ibid., p. 48, *et passim.*

5. *The Purple Island,* I, 9, 13.

6. For more details, see Langdale, Chs. IV and V.

7. Phineas Fletcher, *Venus and Anchises, and Other Poems,* ed. Ethel Seaton (Oxford, 1926), p. xxiv. This stanza was excluded from the original published version.

8. This contention finds support in the Sion College Ms. version (Seaton), where Daphnis is Willoughby, but Algon is not Phineas.

9. See Phineas' modified, Latin version entitled "Fusca." The name "Fusca" has been systematically removed from the *Piscatorie Eclogues;* this eclogue was undoubtedly written originally in the Fusca period, 1606 - 10.

10. Douglas Bush, *Prefaces to Renaissance Literature* (Cambridge, 1966), p. 17. Phineas also wrote a number of Latin poems, the main volume of which is *Sylva Poetica* (1633). He often, as in *Locustae* and *Apollyonists,* wrote a work in both languages.

Chapter Six

1. For fuller discussion, see Seaton, p. xxiii, *et passim;* and Langdale, pp. 37ff.

2. Langdale, p. 53, suggests 1612.

3. Cf. *Christ's Victorie and Triumph* and Milton's *Paradise Lost* where history adds significant dimension.

4. For comparative study see Jerome S. Dees, "The Narrator's Voice in *The Faerie Queene, Christ's Victorie and Triumph,* and *The Locusts or Apollyonists,*" (Doct. diss. University of Illinois, 1968) and Harold F. Brooks, "Oldham and Phineas Fletcher: An Unrecognized Source for *Satyrs Upon the Jesuits,*" *Review of English Studies,* 22 (1971), 410 - 22.

Chapter Seven

1. The Opening dialogue of Thirsil and Thenot relates in references, details, and style to both "To my beloved Thenot" and *Christ's Victorie and Triumph,* or 1606 - 08(9).

2. See especially: *The Purple Island,* I, 33; VI, 3; XII, 8 - 9.

3. They are both versions of the Christian story of divine history; eliminating the anatomy cantos from *The Purple Island,* and viewing *Christ's Victorie and Triumph,* as a conclusion of *The Purple Island,* produces something like a chronological version from the fall of man to the New Jerusalem.

4. A number of scholars have suggested the House (Castle) of Alma, *The Faerie Queene,* II, ix - xii, as the source of the conception of *The Purple Island.* Phineas refers to the passage directly: VI, 42 - 52, 58. For cantos VI - XII, the Castle and War, this passage and the *Psychomachia* are probable sources. For the Man-Island, *Purple Island,* I - V, they are probably not. Islands figure in much of Phineas poetry: piscatory Isles, "this Isle" England *(Apollyonists),* Sicily, etc. Island is also a rather obvious nationalistic symbol.

5. R. G. Baldwin, "Phineas Fletcher: His Modern Readers and His Renaissance Ideas," *Philological Quarterly,* XL (1961), 470.

6. G. MacDonald, *England's Antiphon* (New York, 1868), p. 868; E. Sanford, *The Works of the British Poets* (Philadelphia, 1819), Vol. V, p. 92; *Selected Beauties of Ancient English Poetry,* ed. with remarks by Henry Headley, 2 vols. (London, 1787), I, liii - liv. See also, Linda J. F. Redman, "The Purple Island: A Critical Study" (Doct. diss., Oklahoma State University, 1974).

Chapter Eight

1. Most critics state or assume that he had done his major work by 1615; some even claim 1608 - 12.

2. The prose works are extant only in first editions.

3. Langdale, pp. 81 - 104; quotations, pp. 89, 93.

4. The date is problematic; from style and borrowings from other datable poems, 1610 - 15 seems very possible.

Chapter Nine

1. H. E. Cory, "Spenser, The School of the Fletchers, and Milton," *University of California Publications in Modern Philology,* II, 5 (1912), 311 - 73.

2. Cory, p. 314; see also M. M. Mahood, *Poetry and Humanism* (Oxford, 1950; rpt. New York, 1967), 171 - 2.

3. On the coterie, school, influence, Cory, Langdale, and Grosart offer most evidence and names, but see also Grundy, p. 186, and Chalmers, XXI, p. 146. Grosart adds Henry Peacham, *Period of Mourning* (1613), William Habington, *Castara* (1635), Fuller, Herrick, Gray, Collings, and E. A. Poe. For John Oldham's borrowings from Phineas see note 4, Ch. 6.

4. Winstanley. *Lives of the most famous English Poets* (London, 1687), p. 159. Walton, *The Complete Angler* (London, 1653), pp. 175 - 76; Quarles, "To the Ingenious Composer of this Pastorall . . ." Prefatory to *The Purple Island*.

5. *Selected Works of the British Poets: Chaucer to Jonson*, ed. Robert Southey (London, 1831), p. 807. *The Sacred Classics*, eds. Rev. R. Cattermole and Rev. H. Stebbing (London, 1835), Vol. 21, p. 69.

6. *A Complete Edition of the Poets of Great Britain*, ed. R. Anderson (Edinburgh, 1793), Vol. IV, pp. 378 - 80.

7. *The Spenser of his Age, being Selected Poetry from the Works of Phineas Fletcher*, ed. & introd. by Walter Jerrold (London, 1905), p. 13. Chalmers, Vol. VI, p. 54.

8. Robert A. Willmott, *Lives of the Sacred Poets* (London, 1834), p. 27.

9. D. C. Shelden, "The Complete Poems of Giles Fletcher, the Younger" (Doct. diss. University of Wisconsin, 1938), p. 26.

10. R. G. Baldwin, "Phineas Fletcher: His Modern Readers and His Renaissance Ideas," *Philological Quarterly*, XL (1961), 475.

11. *Seventeenth-Century Prose and Poetry*, eds. A. M. Witherspoon and F. J. Warnke, 2nd ed. (New York, 1963). W. J. Courthope, *A History of English Poetry* (London, 1903), vol. 3, p. 142.

12. Langdale, pp. 166 - 67; Grundy, pp. 202 - 03.

13. Grundy, p. 181. See also Cory, p. 120, and H. E. G. Rope, "Giles Fletcher," *The Month*, II (1932), 14.

14. That these poems reveal an impressive side of Phineas' talent is made clear by the anonymous reviewer of the Seaton edition for the *London Times:* "And he is so musical and adroit a poet, so deft with his little tricks of internal rhyme and of repetition of words and phrases to secure tenderness or emphasis, that the reader cannot but surrender to his 'litle, litle pipe' and carry away its tunes in his head," Anon., "Phineas Fletcher," *[London] Times Literary Supplement* (Aug. 12, 1926), 535.

Selected Bibliography

PRIMARY SOURCES

Works by Giles Fletcher

A Poem in *Sorrowes Joy. Or, A Lamentation for our late deceased Soveraigne Elizabeth, with a triumph for the prosperous succession of our gratious King, James*. Cambridge, England: Legat, 1603.

A Poem in *Epicedium Cantabrigiense, In obitum immaturum, semperque deflendum, Henrici, Illustrissimi Principis Walliae*. Cambridge, England: Legge, 1612.

Christs Victorie and Triumph. Cambridge, England: 1610

Christs Victorie and Triumph. Cambridge, England: Cambridge University Press 1632.

Christ's Victory and Triumph. Cambridge, England: Cambridge University Press 1640.

Complete Poems. Edited by Alexander Grosart. London, Chatto & Windus 1876.

The Reward of the Faithfull. London, n.p., 1623.

Poetical Works of Giles and Phineas Fletcher. Edited by Frederick S. Boas. Cambridge, England: Cambridge University Press, 1908.

"The Complete Poems of Giles Fletcher, the Younger," ed., D. C. Shelden. Doct. diss. University of Wisconsin, 1938.

Works by Phineas Fletcher

A Poem in *Sorrowes Joy. Or, A Lamentation for our late deceased Soveraigne Elizabeth, with a triumph for the prosperous succession of our gratious King, James*. Cambridge, England: Legat, 1603.

A *Poem in Epicedium Cantabrigiense, In obitum immaturum, semperque deflendum, Henrici, Illustrissimi Principis Walliae*. Cambridge, England: Legge, 1612.

Brittain's Ida. Ascribed to Edmund Spenser. London: n.p., 1628.

A Father's Testament. London: n.p., 1670.

Joy In Tribulation. London: n.p., 1632.

Locustae vel pietas Jesuitica. Cambridge, England: Cambridge University Press, 1627.

Piscatory Eclogues with Poetical Miscellanies. Edinburgh: n.p., 1771.

Poems. Edited by Alexander Grosart. Privately printed, 1869.

Poetical Works of Giles and Phineas Fletcher. Edited by Frederick S. Boas. Cambridge, 1908.

The Purple Island, or the Isle of Man: Together with Piscatorie Eclogs and

157

Other Poeticall Miscellanies. Cambridge: England; Cambridge University Press, 1633.

Sicelides. London: England; Cambridge University Press 1631.

Sylva Poetica. Cambridge England: Cambridge University Press, 1633.

Venus and Anchises and other Poems. Edited by Ethel Seaton. Oxford: England; Oxford University Press, 1926.

The Way to Blessednes. London: n.p., 1632.

SECONDARY SOURCES

BALDWIN, R. G. "Phineas Fletcher: His Modern Readers and His Renaissance Ideas." *Philological Quarterly*, X (1961), 462 - 75. Useful review of some historical criticism and views.

BOAS, F. S. *The Poetical Works of Giles and Phineas Fletcher.* Cambridge, England: Cambridge University Press, 1908. Invaluable scholarship and editorial accuracy.

CORY, H. E. "Spenser, The School of the Fletchers, and Milton." *University of California Publications in Modern Philology*, II, 5 (1912), 311 - 73. An excellent relating of the three in the title; useful on members of Fletcher coterie.

COURTHOPE, W. J. *A History of English Poetry.* 6 vols. New York: Columbia University Press, 1895 - 1910. Very balanced literary historical treatment of the Fletchers; relates them accurately to their contemporaries.

GROSART, ALEXANDER B. *The Complete Poems of Giles Fletcher.* London: Chatto & Windus, 1876. Seminal for references, biographical information, and miscellaneous scholarship.

————. *The Poems of Phineas Fletcher.* London; Fuller Worthies Library, 1869. Invaluable for commentary, notes, and miscellany; critically biased as with Giles.

GRUNDY, JOAN. *The Spenserian Poets.* London: Edward Arnold 1969. The most recent lengthy study of the Fletchers is very good (balanced criticism).

LANGDALE, A. B. *Phineas Fletcher: Man of Letters, Science, and Divinity.* New York: Columbia University Press, 1937. The single most valuable biographical study. A storehouse of information about Phineas Fletcher and family.

MAHOOD, M. M. *Poetry and Humanism.* Oxford, England; Oxford University Press, 1950. Reissued 1967. Scholarly criticism of excellent quality but regrettably short on quantity.

SEATON, ETHEL. *Venus and Anchises, and Other Poems.* Oxford, England; Oxford University Press, 1926. The Sion Ms. which she discovered; her notes are essential to any serious study of Phineas Fletcher.

Index

(The works of Giles Fletcher, Jr. and Phineas Fletcher are listed under their names)

159

DATE DUE			

DEMCO 38-297